Just One More Day

In loving memory of my beloved mother...

A remembrance of the last best year.

By Sharon Riche

Dedicated to my beloved mother, Bernice Elbaum

June 13, 1940 - June 7, 1990

"I could search the whole world over,

As far to the sky of blue,

But, I know I'll never find another YOU."

The Seekers (partially...)

Introduction

I never intended to write this book, but just as the chance of fate took my mother, so this book unintentionally evolved out of fear and deep loss.

On July 4th, 1990, exactly twenty seven days after my mother's passing, I was a twenty-four year old bride on my honeymoon in Hawaii. That evening, I was alone, sitting on a chair on a hotel balcony. As I peered out into the warm darkness, I could hear fireworks going off in the distance. I closed my eyes and breathed in the intoxicating and complex aromas of the tropical island. It was beautiful and I thought of how much beauty there was on this earth.

I wondered if my mother was experiencing this moment in time with me. I pondered "where is my mother now?" Is she here with me being caressed by the gentle warm breeze, and feeling what I felt? I suddenly felt so sad that she had been cheated out of life, that her life was cut so short. There was finality in the knowledge that she would never experience such beauty again.

During the honeymoon and for a time afterwards, I searched for signs of her presence, her spirit, her ghost, but found none.

When I returned to work, people would ask me how my father was doing, or some would say, "Oh, you're lucky you have a husband now". It made me feel as if they felt a husband could replace the loss of a mother. Nobody mentioned my mother. I felt like I could not express my grief and sadness in any tangible way. I felt as if I was not validated in being a grieving daughter because of my father's loss and because I was newly married with a husband. I began to fear that I would forget my mother and her memory would fade in time.

I began to call her phone hoping to get an answer but knowing I would not. I would climb the stairs of her house believing I would see her in her room, but knowing I would not. I would sit in her closet, close my eyes and smell her clothes, knowing I would never smell her again. To feel close to her, I would put on her sweaters that she knitted and wore. I would stare at my hands, which strongly resembled her hands, sticking out of the sleeves. I would put on her shoes, knowing I would never walk with her again.

When I was twenty-one and my mother was three years into her cancer, I went with my parents to their best friend's house for Passover. The husband of the couple had passed away from lung cancer and during the Seder, nobody mentioned him. On the drive home my mom said that she thought it was sad that between his wife and children nobody talked about him. My mother's sadness made me realize that she was afraid of being forgotten if G-d forbid she didn't survive her illness.

I was now twenty-four years old and my mother was gone. Nobody else seemed to be talking about my mother anymore. I had a revelation that my mother's fear that she would be forgotten could indeed come true. My mother's fear became my fear. I felt that I now needed to record the moments in time of my mother's passing before they drifted away forever.

I began to look in my calendar to see how things unfolded as they did. I soon found myself writing the moments down, what I remembered and thought. I wrote these memories down so I wouldn't forget them.

I knew that I could not bring my mother back but in writing things down, maybe I could have something that I could hold in my hands, something tangible like her sweaters to keep her memory alive. It became cathartic for me.

It became comforting for me.

Like unseen fireworks heard in the distance, echoing over a silent ocean.

This is a work of non-fiction.

Certain names have been changed to protect the privacy of others.

December 7, 1989

As I was driving up the steep hill to my house I had a very calm feeling within me. I thought, "I am so happy." For me, this was not an ordinary realization. I wasn't able to truly feel this way in such a long time. I reminisced back on my days at U.C.S.B. (University of California Santa Barbara) the chronic insomnia, the stress, the insecurities, the fear of my future, the depression. It was as if I was someone else for I could not relate to that person anymore. My life was now so different. Things could not have been better for me that day and time. I found true love and happiness with Tom and our wedding was only six months away. I was awaiting that day with such excitement. I finally found a degree of content with my new job at ABC. I enjoyed my family and truly cared for my friends. Life was almost perfect. It was wonderful to feel happiness at last.

December 16, 1989

I was so excited this morning. Caren and Sofia were coming over to order their bridesmaids dresses. That will be four down and five to go I thought to myself. Another thing to check off my "to do for the wedding" list.

Before I started getting ready Mom called me into her bedroom. She was lying on her bed resting. I sat on the edge of the bed next to her where I always sat when we talked. As always she looked so beautiful. I always admired her gray-blue eyes. They looked at me so lovingly; there was a sweet innocence about them. I was so proud that even without make-up and in her illness and chemotherapy, she was always a sight of beauty. I knew she would age gracefully. I just hoped I would look as young as she when I turned forty-nine.

"Listen," she said, "I have something I want to ask you." I figured it was about the bridesmaids dresses. She went on to say, "Would you ever consider moving up the wedding?" "Why?" I asked. "Well," she answered, "what if I don't make it to the wedding?" she said with a cute smile.

I was surprised at her for being so silly. Of course she was going to make it to the wedding. I thought she was getting a little too worried. I asked what Dr. Averon said and he said she would not only be at the wedding, she would live to see her grandchildren. So I replied, "Why would you think this then?" She said seriously but like a little child, "If I don't make it to the wedding, I don't want you to be mad at me." I started laughing and said, "Of course I won't be mad at you! But, I know you're going to make it so there's nothing to worry about."

Mom said, "You know that if I'm not here, Dad can't make a wedding. I want you to realize that." I said with a smile, "I'm not worried. Nothing's going to happen." "Okay, fine," she answered. "If you're not worried then I'm not worried. If that's what you want then we won't move up the wedding. As long as you promise not to be mad at me if I'm not here."

I thought she was being so cute and. funny with her silly thoughts. I wondered why out of nowhere she was having these fears. I asked, "Do you really think you're not going to make it?" She said, "I don't know. I'm scared." She started crying. I hugged her as she was lying down and we both cried. She sobbed, "I love you so much."

I had only known Mom for her strength and optimism throughout her illness. It frightened me that for the first time I was seeing her fear. This wasn't like her. I wondered if there was more she wasn't telling me. I said she would be fine and nothing was going to happen. After all, she was a fighter. She survived her illness for five and a half years so that made her a survivor.

Nothing could happen now.

Suddenly I was scared too. I thought about that letter that Gloria wrote to Mom about a month after Matt and Tera's wedding. At the wedding Mom had thought she beat it. She was in remission. But this letter frightened me. Gloria wrote, "Keep your spirits up, just enjoy Sharon's wedding as much as you enjoyed Matt's." I didn't understand it. Now it was a little more clear. The cancer was back, but this time it was different. How bad could it be for Mom to not think she would make it? I was so afraid but too hopeful to give up on her. She beat it before, she would beat it again.

I wanted to stay with Mom longer but Caren and Sofia were going to be over any minute. I didn't want to leave her. She said, "Go get ready." I couldn't move. Bridesmaids dresses just didn't seem to matter anymore.

Caren rang the bell and I still didn't even begin to get ready. She could see that I was crying and asked with concern what was wrong. I filled her in as I got ready real fast. Caren was freaking out. When I answered the door for Sofia the first thing that came out of her mouth was, "Dave and I broke up." It looked like she had been crying. I asked what happened and she gave me the whole story. She didn't even notice that there was something wrong with me, so I told her. She realized that her problems were petty compared to mine. Over lunch, Sofia and Caren urged me to move up the wedding. I kept saying that moving up the wedding was being negative and I didn't want to give my mom the impression that I was giving up hope. Moving the wedding up would only cause my parents more stress. It was too much of a hassle to re-plan every detail and everything was booked. Nothing would be ready on time. Caren and Sofia begged me to move it up.

Caren said, "If we have to we will buy our bridesmaids dresses off the rack somewhere." Sofia added, "Who cares if things aren't perfect. Sharon, your family is so special. I've never seen such a close family that cares about each other so much like yours. You can't get married without your mother there. It will be devastating for you. Why take that risk?" I said the wedding was only six months away so what difference would a few months make? Mom would be the same either way. Sofia said, "Sharon, I've seen these things happen before. Cancer can change things and make things happen very quickly. I just don't want to see this happen to you. If you move it up you are safe."

Caren and Sofia were so persistent. They warned me that I was making a big mistake not moving it up. They offered to help with whatever I needed to do to reschedule all the arrangements. I stood my ground. I felt so strongly that Mom would be there. She fought the disease for five and a half years and never got worse. Why would she get worse in six months? I thought Caren and Sofia were exaggerating and being pessimistic of her fate. I appreciated them for caring and being so concerned. But, that was not the end of it.

Each time I talked to them after that day, they begged me again and again to move the date up. Mom discussed this dilemma with Tom and the whole family. Everyone was crying. Mom only shed a few tears. She was always the strongest.

It seemed as if we had just had this exact same discussion not too long ago. I remembered it so well. It was right after the first night of Rosh Hashanah services two years ago. We had the big "what if" talk. The dreaded "what if Mom doesn't make it" talk. I was scared then but not as scared as I was now. Mom always told us that Dad should never be alone. She wanted him to remarry and we had to be supportive and nice to his new "bride." Then she would joke about it and tell Dad that he better not give her all her diamonds.

Dad never laughed at those remarks. None of us were laughing now.

We all agreed to keep the date as it was. Matt firmly thought we should just leave it as is. Tom thought changing the date was a bad premonition. It showed that we thought Mom wouldn't make it. I also thought changing the date showed a negative attitude. I just thought the idea of Mom not making it was so far-fetched. Mom said, "I already talked to Sharon about this. We had a good cry. She knows that if I don't make it, Dad can't make a wedding, right, Sharon?" I said I understood. But, nothing was going· to happen. We all agreed that everything would be fine and we would be married on June 24th as planned. There was no doubt in my mind that Mom would not be there.

January 9, 1990

As she always did every week Mom was awaiting lab and x-ray results from Dr. Averon. As I was walking up the stairs I heard her on the phone. I sat on the second step on the staircase so I could listen. Mom said, "No, I didn't hurt myself." (playing tennis or on the cruise that they went on over New Year's) Mom had been having excruciating pain in the back of her neck to the extent that it made her scream each time it hurt. Dr. Averon said the x-ray showed that she had a fractured vertebrae. Since this was so peculiar Dr. Averon asked Mom again if she was sure she didn't hurt herself. She replied in a worried tone, "I'm positive." This made the doctor conclude that there must be cancer activity in the back of her neck and this could mean she had disease tissue in her skull. I kept hearing Mom say, "Oh, dear God" each time she replied to whatever Dr. Averon was saying.

She then said, "So what does this mean? What now? I see…" She hung up and told Dad everything. "Sharon," she called out. "You can come in sweetie." It was so typical of Mom to sense me on the staircase listening. I came in to their bedroom. Mom said the cancer spread more to her bones and was now in the skull. They were going to start radiation and continue her chemotherapy. I couldn't believe this was happening.

February 5, 1990

Uncle Nolan and Aunt Barb were in town staying with us for five days. Nolan was celebrating his 60th birthday.

Nolan really treated Mom like his baby sister. I always loved how he called her, "Bern." I came home from work and they were sitting at the kitchen table with Mom. To my surprise, Mom was wearing a neck brace. "What's that?" I asked. She said with a grin, "Do you like my new necklace?" I just could not laugh. "What is it for?" I asked. Mom said she had to wear it from now on since her bones were so fragile. Naturally this meant she couldn't play tennis anymore and had to be very cautious. It was so hard to believe that she had just won a tennis tournament a month ago and danced on a cruise six weeks ago. I could tell the neck brace was so uncomfortable and unnatural for her. It must have felt terribly awkward.

Mom's sense of humor never ceased to amaze me. She asked me to get her that rhinestone "B" initial pin that she probably wore in the seventies or something. She stuck it on her neck brace to make it look nice. It actually made her neck brace look more like a piece of jewelry. That was really Mom's character. I was so proud of her. She always found a way to make the best out of any given situation. I admired her attitude.

February 7, 1990

Since I had told Sandy that Mom was doing a lot of creative visualization and was reading "Love, Medicine, and Miracles" by Bernie S. Siegel a second time, Sandy went out and did some research herself. Sandy gave me some self-help books and tapes on guided imagery to give to Mom. They seemed wonderful. Mom was so excited when I gave them to her. "How sweet of her!" she said with surprise. "She didn't have to do this, how nice!" Moms eyes watered when she read the card Sandy had enclosed. I asked if I could read it. It said, "May you find these helpful in guiding you in your healing." I hoped they would work. Mom was willing to try anything. I admired her courage so much. But, I was so scared for her.

February 9, 1990

Mom had a nice time as always with Uncle Nolan and Aunt Barb. They were leaving early the next morning.

February 10, 1990

I awoke early this morning to Mom's screams. At first I thought I was dreaming. Mom kept screaming, "No! Don't go!" She started crying hysterically and wouldn't let go of Nolan. I just realized she was saying good-bye to Nolan. Did she think she was never going to see him again? Was this the last time she would ever hug him? I could not understand why she was screaming. He was coming back in four months for the wedding. Of course, she was going to miss him, but she was out of control, not letting him go.

When I got home from work I asked Mom why she was screaming. She looked so sad and said, "Oh, I just got emotional." I could tell she was keeping her feelings from me. I just prayed that she wasn't losing hope. Of course she would see Nolan again.

February 14, 1990

Tom and I went out to dinner for Valentine's Day. I got home kind of late. Mom came into my room. "Happy Valentine's Day!" I wished her. I could tell she was just sleeping. She looked sad. "Tera had a miscarriage," she said with regret and distress in her voice. "Oh, no!" I just kept saying over and over again. Mom got into my bed. I just laid next to her saying, "Oh, no" over and over. I asked how it happened. Mom said the baby stopped growing. Tera went to the hospital today. First I felt awful for Matt and Tera.

They wanted this baby so bad for Mom. We all did. They could try again in six weeks. Tera was eleven weeks pregnant. That meant that Tera and Matt had lost about five months of crucial time. Five months was really nothing to delay having a baby. But, in our case five months was vital for Mom. What also scared me was that Tera's pregnancy gave Mom something to live for, to hold on to. How could she fight for her own life after this loss of life? She was really looking forward to holding this baby.

I looked at Mom laying in my bed. She was curled up in a ball with her eyes closed. She looked so sad. I knew she was thinking just what I was thinking. She was afraid she wouldn't be here for the birth of her first grandchild. I was scared for all of us. Poor Matt and Tera. I called them the next day. Tera said Matt was crying the whole way to work. Even though it wasn't my baby that was lost I could relate to what he was feeling. I wanted to make Mom a grandmother too. Whether it was my baby or Matt's baby I still had a wish to see Mom as a grandmother. It hurt so much and there was nothing any of us could do.

February 18, 1990

Today was Marissa's surprise sweet sixteen party at Braemar Country Club. It was pouring rain when we got out of the car. I held Mom carefully and took small steps as we walked to the club. I wasn't used to her needing me so much and holding on to me for support. But, it felt good that she needed me so.

The party was real nice. Tera drove Marissa there letting her think it was my shower. Tera even got me a shower gift to fool Marissa but, Marissa knew the whole time. I felt so old being with all those cute little fifteen and sixteen year-olds.

I remembered my sweet sixteen vividly. The palm reader that was there I could have sworn was the same woman I had at my sweet sixteen. She predicted that I would break up with my boyfriend Jeremy and I thought she was out of her mind and knew nothing. Sure enough we broke up two months later.

Mom and I had our palms read. The palm reader said Mom would have a long life. Mom was so happy with her prediction. She seemed to really believe it. Victoria, on the other hand was terrified to even have her palm read. She said she was afraid of what she would say. She was in remission but ever since she was diagnosed with cancer she was a nervous wreck and petrified. Mom was always brave and thought the best. Tera was so depressed about losing the baby she told me she couldn't go through with the poem that we wrote with Jennifer to recite to Marissa. So Jennifer and I recited it without Tera. I felt so terrible for Tera. Marissa loved the poem. Overall, it was a fun day.

February 19, 1990

Mom told me that her cousin Jules got hit by a Mack truck while crossing the street. He was in critical condition and had to get his leg amputated. Poor Roberta. How could something like this happen to such nice people? What a stupid question. That was the way life was.

February 20, 1990

Tom and I had a long talk about his predicament at his job. After a year and a half of hard work and long hours and devotion he finally realized he did not want to be an agent. We explored a lot of alternatives. I was so used to adversity and drastic changes that I wasn't even surprised at how calm I was over all this.

February 23, 1990

After a lot of meetings, thinking, and analyzing, Tom and I decided he would leave the agency business. What a week this had been. Mom's condition worsening, Tera's miscarriage, Jules' accident, and now this. What would happen next?

February 24, 1990

Mom and I went to Paper Pushers to order the wedding invitations. We went through more books just to make sure that the one we picked out was the best one. Dad and Tom definitely liked it but we wanted to be sure so we looked at more. There were two women sitting at the table with us looking through books also. I guess one of them was friendly with the owner. She said to her, "Did you hear Harriet Rosenblum died? I went to her funeral last week, brain cancer." Mom cringed and made a sickened face. I tried to give that woman a dirty look but she didn't see me. She even had the gall to go on and say, "I'm sorry; I know this isn't nice to say about a deceased person but she was a bitch." Mom just ignored her. But, I was very angry at this woman's lack of consideration and decency. Did it ever occur to them that other people who can hear them in a public place might be offended?

I guess not.

February 25, 1990

Mom's neck hurt so much that she couldn't even read in bed anymore. All those self-help books just sat on her nightstand unopened yet yearned to be read by her. It was so frustrating. She couldn't even enjoy curling up with a great book without pain and discomfort.

February 26, 1990

After work I went to AEPhi (my sorority) for Maxine's candle passing. It was beautiful. It reminded me of my pinning. I remembered how proud Mom was at our serenade. She had tears in her eyes the whole time and never stopped smiling. She was so happy Tom and I were pinned because she knew we would soon be engaged. Those were the times to remember.

March 3, 1990

Mom and Dad went out this morning to get Mom a cane. After they left I burst into tears. Mom's physical deterioration was suddenly hitting me. She was becoming physically incompetent, growing weaker and was having trouble walking. The cancer was eating away her bones.

I always saw Mom as such an active person. It was so difficult to accept her in a neck brace and now a cane. It just wasn't right. How was she going to dance at the wedding like this? I felt so awful for her. To be an active person running around one minute and to have it all taken away from you the next must have felt so frustrating. When Mom got home with the cane she showed us how she walked with it and said, "Isn't this nifty?" She said she was going to get a cane in every color to match her outfits. Her sense of humor never died. I admired her strength so much.

March 8, 1990

Mom and I were planning on going to Magic Moments today to look at headpieces. When I was ready to leave Mom was in bed. She said, "I'm so sorry. I feel lousy and I'm so tired. I really want to go but I just don't have the strength sweetie." She was so apologetic and looked so sad that she couldn't go. She felt like she was letting me down. She said Kaye offered to go with me. I said it wasn't the same thing. I needed my mother with me. Mom said with frustration, "I know, I really want to go with you, but I just can't."

My heart broke for Mom. She felt guilty for not being there for me and was sad because she was missing out. I tried to not act disappointed but Mom could see right through me. I kept telling her it was okay. We both knew it wasn't. It was sad for both of us.

March 9, 1990

For months Sandy was saying that she wanted to go to Bullock's with Tom and me to register. Finally, we set up a date for her to meet us after work tonight. She met us at Crate and Barrel. We were there for about a half hour just looking at everything. We decided to come back another time and maybe not even register there. Then we went to Bullock's. We went from one section to another wandering around and looking at a million different things instead of concentrating and focusing on one major thing at a time. We each had drastically different taste.

Sandy kept telling me to get what I liked as opposed to what I'm used to at home. What she didn't understand was that I loved Mom's taste and Mom always respected my opinion when it came to decorating. We always made choices together so we acquired the same taste together. I really wished Mom could have gone with me. We were there for over an hour and registered for one lousy wooden salad bowl. I was very frustrated.

We finally came up with the brilliant idea of asking for help. It turned out that Tom knew the salesperson. Of course he did. He knew everybody. They went to Beverly together. He was a friend of Paul's. This guy wasn't too much of a help. But, we did get other things accomplished.

Sandy went crazy in the linen department. She bought Tom and I the extra huge California King size sheets for our bed. She got us about three sheets and some pillow cases too. Then she went nuts with the towels. She had bought us some towels from Robinson's and was having a ball looking at every single towel in the department comparing to the ones she got at Robinson's. Then she wanted to buy us a bunch of pillows too, but I told her not too. Tom was going out of his mind. He wanted to leave the minute we got there. I thought it was fun. It was so sweet and generous of Sandy to buy us all those things. It was nothing new.

March 15, 1990

I went to Magic Moments after work to try on the headpiece that Carolyn had made for someone else that she thought I would like. I tried it on and studied myself in the mirror but I was lost. I needed Mom's opinion. I was so surprised when I saw Jody there. She was picking out her bridesmaids dresses. She ordered her gown from Renee Strauss. Her wedding was in August. I felt silly talking to her in a head piece wearing my clothes from work. Her mother was with her of course. I was jealous. I felt funny that they saw me alone in a bridal shop without my mother. I had such pride that I didn't want anyone to think that Mom took no interest in my choosing my head piece. She felt terrible that she was missing out on this. I wanted to say why she wasn't with me but I really wasn't close enough with Jody to explain. I just let it go.

I tried on some more headpieces but I became even more confused. How could I go home and explain to Mom what these looked like? She had to be there to see for herself. I was so depressed. Carolyn gave me some more ideas. She put together two beautiful combs and put them on the crown of my head. They looked perfect. Carolyn said she would put them on a wire with loops for the combs. She would have it ready in two weeks. She was so helpful. I know she was doing this because she was friends with Mom. I felt a little better.

March 17, 1990

Mom kept telling me to go register for more things. My first shower that Kaye was giving me was only two months away. Mom felt terrible that she was too weak to go with me. I went to Robinson's today without her. I was lost. I had no clue what else to register for. Tera said she would go with me soon. She would be a great help.

March 19, 1990

Gloria flew in from New York to stay with us to spend time with Mom. I love Gloria like a second Mom. I guess because Gloria was Mom's best friend in the whole world for over thirty years she and Mom were the same person to me. I found it odd that Gloria spontaneously flew in especially without Carl. They were both going to be in town in three months for the wedding so why would she come in for a week right now? I hoped this didn't mean that Gloria knew something that I didn't.

Gloria and Mom had so much fun together. They watched old home movies from over twenty-five years ago. Gloria and Mom were so cute back then with their pointy rhinestone sixties sunglasses and beehive hairdos. Matt and I were on the floor laughing at Mom and Gloria playing in the hotel pools with me, Matt, Nina and John as babies. Gloria was screaming at how big her thighs were and Mom was screaming over how skinny she was. Mom and Gloria laughed at themselves and reminisced on all those great times they had with their babies at the Zoo, Disneyland, San Diego and Palm Springs.

As Gloria always did when she was visiting L.A., she and Mom went on a huge shopping spree on Rodeo. Gloria came back with the most adorable outfits for her new granddaughter Ashley.

Gloria showed me everything she bought. When she showed me the cute little outfits she got Ashley, Mom smiled at them but with a sad face. I knew what she was thinking.

March 20, 1990

Gloria spent most of her stay sitting in the chair by Mom's bed while Mom laid in bed and they talked for hours and hours. Gloria was leaving in a couple of days. Mom said like a little kid, "I don't want you to go." Gloria said, "I love this. I could stay forever. I don't want to go either." But, she had to go.

March 21, 1990

Gloria confided in Tom and me. She said she was very worried about Dad. She didn't like the way he was reacting to Mom and he needed help. She said, "This could go on for years." Later, Tom said it was a great sign that Gloria said, "This could go on for years," meaning Gloria thought Mom would live "for years." That gave me a lot of hope, because I knew Gloria knew the truth.

March 22, 1990

After work Tera went with me to Robinson's to help me register. Mom joked, "I don't know why you're registering. You're never going to use all those things. You don't even know how to use half that stuff." Ha ha. I was so glad Tera went with me. She knew exactly what I would need.

I drove Tera home. We talked in my car in front of her house with the car running. We were just saying good-bye but we ended up talking for what seemed like an eternity. I finally turned the engine off. Tera expressed her concern for Dad. She said he wasn't preparing himself and wanted to find a support group for him. She thought we could all go first to check it out for ourselves before suggesting it to him. Then we would go with him his first time.

Dad would never do therapy I told her.

Tera said, "When Mom dies, Dad has to be ready." I thought to myself, "when" Mom dies. What did she mean by "when?" Why didn't Tera say, "If" Mom dies?

What was she getting at? I simply asked, "What do you mean? You think she's going to die?" Tera answered, "Mom's not doing well at all Sharon. Her coughing is getting worse, it's in her lungs, and she's just not getting better." I asked, "Well, when do you think she'll die?" My voice was trembling. Tera said, "Probably about six months."

I felt a huge lump in my throat. I demanded to know who told her this. She said the Havarah had been talking about it and basically she just wasn't doing well so they all figured she had about six months. Dr. Averon never gave anyone that figure. He never gave Mom a prognosis. He said she would live to see her grandchildren.

But, Tera had a point. Mom wasn't doing well at all. She was getting worse. Before I could finish my next sentence I burst into tears. I tried to say, "But, I just don't understand this. I thought she was going to beat this."

I couldn't stop crying. Tera held my head and touched my face. Six months was too soon. It wasn't enough time. I wasn't ready. I would probably never be ready, but six months? I couldn't accept that. I needed more time. This just couldn't be happening. Six months was in September. How could Mom miss the High Holy Days? Ever since she got sick she would cry at the end of each service, especially Rosh Hashanah. We would all cry and hug each other. Mom would say something to me like, "Good Yontiff. I love you so much."

I always knew that she was wishing me only good health for that year. And her tears only meant one thing and that was her fear of not being with us for the next year. Mom made those holidays special for me. Her will to live gave me something to pray for and hold on to and gave meaning to the New Year. The endings of those services were the rare occasions that I would see Mom cry and it always made me feel so close to her. I could feel her fear and it made me scared for her. The thought of not celebrating Rosh Hashanah and Yom Kippur with Mom was incomprehensible. I wanted one last holiday season with her. I never imagined that last year's holidays would be the last with Mom. That word "last" gave me a sick feeling. I pictured myself in six months. There was so much to look forward to.

How could I enjoy setting up my apartment without Mom? How could I live in my own brand new place without Mom visiting and giving me decorating ideas? I was so excited about shocking her by serving her dinner in my own new home for a change. That would be so much fun.

And what about Matt and Tera? They were going to try again soon to get pregnant. How could Mom not be there to hold her first grandchild? This made no sense.

I told Tom what Tera had said. Tom said angrily, "What do they know! They're not doctors! She is fighting this and she'll make it. I just know it." Maybe Tom was right. After all, Dr. Averon thought she would live longer than six months. Whenever Mom saw him she would remind him of my wedding. I just had to remember what he said when Mom asked if she would live to see my wedding. He said, "You will enjoy your daughter's wedding and you will even live to see your grandchildren." It just had to be true. I wasn't giving up as long as Mom wasn't. I still had to have hope for her. The wedding was only three months away and she would be there with many more days ahead of her. She just had to be.

March 25, 1990

Tom and I went to see Rabbi Shuman today. I told him about Mom. He looked very concerned. I said confidently, "Everything will be fine. She'll be okay." He replied, "No, everything will not be okay. I want you to prepare yourselves. Things happen very quickly with cancer and people go very fast." He really scared me, but then I thought he was being negative.   I didn't want to hear what he had to say. I know he was trying to warn me and prepare me for the worst. But he didn't know Mom like I did. She was so strong and had such a will to survive.

Nothing would stop her from being at our wedding.

March 26, 1990

Mom asked me what I wanted for my birthday. I said I just wanted her. She smiled. Since I wanted to see "Starlight Express" Mom said she would treat Tom and me to the tickets. I was excited, but I still only wanted her health for my birthday.

March 27, 1990

I went to AAA today to get Mom a handicapped parking permit application. All she needed to do was have Dr. Averon approve it. When I brought it home to her she seemed happy about it. Dad seemed upset about it, but I knew it was a great idea to enable Mom to go out more.

March 29, 1990

I went into Magic Moments after work to try on the headpiece. It looked beautiful. The only problem was I was confused about the poof of the veil. That's when I really needed Mom. She was very into the poof and knew exactly what would look nice on me. I couldn't make this decision without her. There had to be some way she could come in. Maybe she would feel stronger soon.

March 30, 1990

Today was my birthday, but as usual I felt nothing. Big deal, I am 24 I thought. But I was in the exact place I dreamed of being at age 24. I was getting married. I was perfectly content knowing that all I was doing for my birthday which happened to fall on a Friday night was having dinner at home with my family.

I thought I would have plenty of time for a manicure after work. I ran a little late. When I got home everybody was there. Before I could answer where I was Mom said, "I know where you were. You got your nails done; they look nice."

She amazed me. She knew me so well. She was such a "mother." I prayed with all my heart that this birthday would not be the last I would share with her.

In the back of my mind I feared it was.

March 31, 1990

Mom went with me to look at wedding rings. We went to two jewelers. One was recommended by Linda at Magic Moments and the other place was where Mom went with Matt when he bought Tera pearls. I was so happy Mom made the strength to go with me. She knew so much about quality and what looked nice on my hand and what didn't. She was so meticulous. She knew what questions to ask the jeweler and knew a high quality diamond from a low one.

We looked at about three that really caught my eye. There were a few things I liked but like Mom said, I had to love it. So far, there was nothing that I absolutely loved.

April 9, 1990

Mom was losing a lot of weight. The way she put it to Sandy was, "I'm losing weight in all the wrong places." She was losing her shape and form. For the first time ever I found her to be insecure about how she looked. Losing her hair was one thing because she could wear a wig and she had been dealing with that for six years already. But losing such an abundant amount of weight probably made her feel out of control with her body. It was Passover so I was fixing her hair for the Seder. I loved doing her hair and make-up. It was moments like those that made our relationship so special. I really felt like her only daughter. I loved the cute smile she would give me after I was finished.

Whether she looked great or not she would say, "Rad! Thanks!" Today, she wasn't feeling too good about herself. I was wearing a snug fitting knit dress that really accentuated my curves. Mom was down about all the weight she lost. She said, "I've lost my shape. Look at you. You're skinny, but you still have a butt, and hips, and a nice shape. I don't have mine anymore. I've lost in all the wrong places. I have no butt." I didn't know what to say because she was right. I wanted to cheer her up so I just said, "Not really, don't let it bother you." But it did. I felt so badly for her. I knew what it was like to feel insecure about my looks. But Mom was never like that. It just wasn't natural.

April 10, 1990

Mom's handicapped parking permit was finally ready. I picked it up. I was bewildered when the expiration date read, "10/10/90" and the permit was for a "temporary disability." At first I was angry. I thought Dr. Averon was saying that Mom had six months to live and she wouldn't need it passed 10/10/90 because she wouldn't be alive. I felt like Mom wasn't being honest with me. I asked her why he only gave her until 10/10/90 and she said, "I don't know. I guess he thinks I won't need it for that long. Hopefully I'll be better by then."

I wanted to believe her but I just couldn't. I was picturing my life six months from now. How could I be married, living in a new apartment, with a new life and not have Mom around? And what about Jennifer's Bat Mitzvah in November? Mom was really looking forward to that. What did this 10/10/90 date mean? Maybe Mom would be better, but I just couldn't see it. I was so scared.

April 14, 1990

Mom and I went for my dress fitting. I couldn't believe it was here. It fit perfectly. Linda was so surprised at how little I was. My measurements came out to be a size 2 and Linda was going to order a size 4 to be safe because this manufacturer ran real small. But, it fit perfectly in the waist and back. The only part that needed altering were of course the hem and the bustle had to be done. Mom and I were thrilled with how the sleeves came out. We were worried because we custom ordered the sleeves and weren't sure how they would look with the dress.

It was gorgeous. Linda said the alterations would be ready in a month. She didn't want me to come in for my final fitting until a few weeks before the wedding just in case I would lose weight. I told her I wouldn't but she didn't agree with me. Mom looked at every detail and asked about a tiny crease on the side of my waist. I would never have noticed it. It was just the texture of the material. But, that was exactly what I needed her there for.

I was so happy she was there.

Mom really liked the head piece. We finally figured out the poof and the veil. Mom wanted a lot of fullness in the back too. She was very picky. It was great.

April 19, 1990

Tom and I made plans to go to San Diego for the weekend. Adam's parents owned a hotel there so the room was free. We hadn't gone away for the weekend in what seemed like forever. When I told Mom she said, "Good, you two need to get away. The poor boy is working so hard." She really surprised me. I thought she would be upset that we were going away. She was actually happy for us.

April 26, 1990

Every time I got home from work I made it a routine to run up to Mom's room to sit with her. I felt such guilt for not doing that all my life. I always enjoyed her company, but I liked to have time to myself right after work. But things were going to change. We talked for a time while she laid in her bed.

"Listen," Mom said, "I really need to know what jewelry of mine you want." She had asked me this before, but I just shrugged it off. I said, "I just want you."

"I'm serious," Mom said. "I really need to know. I want you to have first choice."

It hadn't even entered my mind. She had me try on her diamond rings and bracelet to see how they looked on me. Mom and I had the exact same looking hands and fingernails so it spooked me to look at my hand with her ring on it. I didn't like the feeling I was getting at all.

The most important thing was to divide the jewelry equally by value between Matt, Stephen, and me, so we went over the value of her pendants also. I suggested that Stephen get Mom's engagement ring to give to his future wife. Mom said no way because she was never going to know his future wife and she didn't want her ring being worn by someone she would never know.

Mom had two diamond pendants. One pendant Mom made from Grandma Rose's stone of her engagement ring. I thought it would be a beautiful tradition if I did the same with Mom's engagement ring. Her two carat stone would make an exquisite pendant, which would be sentimental to me. Then I would leave my daughter my engagement stone to make into a pendant.

We sat in silence for a while. I thought of Mom's bridal portrait on the wall behind me. It was a painting of Mom as a bride; she was barely twenty years old, thirty years ago. When I was real little I used to stare at it with admiration and pride hoping to be a bride just like her. "Can I have that picture of you?" I asked her softly. Mom's eyes started to water as she answered, "yes." I would hope Matt and Stephen would understand how much that painting meant to me but I felt better having Mom say it was okay for me to have it. One day I would hang it in my house and have my children admire their grandmother the way I used to as a little girl.

April 27, 1990

Beth, our calligrapher was done with all the envelopes for the invitations. Tom and I had been driving back and forth to her house all week to give her additions, changes, etc. She did them so speedily.

We were getting so excited.

April 28, 1990

Mom and I went downtown today to look for wedding rings. I felt awful because of all the walking Mom had to do. But she was so enthusiastic about finding the perfect ring. We were at Chris's place for such a long time studying about three settings. When Chris brought out another setting we knew it was the one. Mom loved it and was so excited about it. Just for fun we looked next door for rings for Tom.

There were several jewelers and zillions of men's wedding bands to choose from, it was overwhelming.

Mom noticed one for Tom. She studied it. She realized the reason she was so attracted to it was because it was so similar to her own wedding ring. We took down the jeweler and style number.

Maybe one day Tom and I would take a look at it.

April 29, 1990

Mother's day was only two weeks away. I wanted to do something special and out of the ordinary for Mom. Whenever I bought her a gift for her birthday or Mother's Day she would put it away and it was never seen again. I did not want that this year. Especially when I was haunted by the horrifying thought of this being the last Mother's Day she would have.

I cried at the thought of not having a Mom to give something special to on Mother's Day. I wanted to give her something that would inspire her to fight to live. Not that she wasn't fighting with all her might as it was. I wanted to give her something uplifting and to make her feel like the best mother that ever lived.

I always felt good whenever she cried over the Mother's Day cards I gave her every year. I wanted to give her something in my own words this time. That's when I started working on a poem just for her. There were traces of tears on all my rough drafts. To see my feelings for her on paper hurt and felt good at the same time. I thought of how beautiful the poem would be if it were surrounded by pictures of her with her children. I imagined this collage to be sitting right beside her bed on her nightstand. That way, when she was lying in bed all day and night she would constantly be reminded of how much we needed and loved her. I knew she had a strong will to live and was never going to give up. But, I just hoped this special gift could make a difference in her destiny. I felt it was all I could do at this time.

April 30, 1990

Mom and I started stuffing the invitations. The toughest part was sealing them. Mom was such a perfectionist. She couldn't stand the air bubbles that were left on the seal. So she experimented with the "not so important" guests.

People like Tom's friends wouldn't even notice something like that. Mom could just tell by the person's name that it was one of Tom's friends. She cracked me up. She picked up Michael Solomon's envelope. "He doesn't know anything, right?" she asked as she was about to do his invitation. She was hysterical.

She insisted on doing her own people. She didn't like the way I was doing it. She could see the air pockets and they were driving her crazy. We tried a glue stick followed by pressing them with a huge book but since the lining was a silver, reflective, slippery textured material, it was difficult. Mom was determined to seal them perfectly.

May 1, 1990

We sent all the New Yorkers out today. It was totally hitting me. We were actually getting married in less than eight weeks. Mom was also getting so excited. She would be at our wedding. I just knew she would.

May 4, 1990

Mom, Dad, Tom and I were planning to meet with our video guy tonight. Since it was in Sherman Oaks I stopped by the piano music store to buy the sheet music for our first dance, "Always." I wanted to play it for Dad since he wasn't sure how it went and also just in case Jim Cole, our band leader needed it, which I highly doubted. We had a date to meet with him May 9 to go over the details.

I was not happy with the video guy at all. Mom was pretty upset too. Just like me, Mom wanted everything perfect. Of course Dad did as well, but Mom amazed me. I could tell she was feeling lousy yet she still stood up to the video guy and told him exactly what was on her mind. We went to dinner afterwards. It was a nice evening.

May 5, 1990

Mom and Kaye were going to Nicole's Boutique to get Mom's gown for the wedding fitted. I told Mom I really wanted to go with them. That morning, I had to get all the materials I needed for Mom's gift. I went to three different places to find the perfect mat and frame. I was going crazy because I had to get home on time to go with Mom and Kaye.

Unfortunately, these art stores weren't open on Sundays so I had to get these things today. When I got home Mom was waiting by the stairs. Before she could ask where I was I said, "Sorry, it's a surprise." Just by the expression on her face I could see curiosity, yet satisfaction with my reply.

The gown was absolutely stunning. Mom looked gorgeous. It was as if the gown was made for her. Her body and even her haircut were perfect for the style of the dress. I was so excited to show her off at the wedding. I was so proud of her. I pictured Mom and Dad walking me down the aisle and having people admire Mom as they walked me down. She was so beautiful and looked so sexy in this dress.

Afterwards we went next door to Erik's to look at shoes. Mom told Kaye she was leaving me her shoes. I looked at Mom and told her, "I'd rather have you." She just grinned.

When we got back in the car Kaye fastened Mom's seat belt. "We don't want to lose you now, since we just bought your dress," Kaye joked. I thought of how Mom was looking forward to Jennifer's Bat Mitzvah. She was planning on wearing her gown for that as well.

Kaye asked about Julia. She and Stephen were becoming real serious. Mom said "I don't know why, but I'm just not nice to her. She's so attentive to me. Whenever she hears me cough she runs in my room and offers to refill my water bottle. She always comes in my room to see if I need anything."

"Well, that's very nice." Kaye said. "Why aren't you nice to her?" "I don't know," Mom said. "I guess I don't like Stephen having a relationship at his age."   I knew how much it hurt Stephen that Mom did not like Julia. I hoped they would make peace for Stephen's sake. I was surprised Mom was so conscious of how she was not nice to Julia. At least she could admit it. It was hard to deal with. Stephen was her baby.

May 6, 1990

I had an emotional talk with Tom and Sandy this morning. I told Sandy everything I had told Tom about my childhood that nobody else ever knew about. We talked about the deep insecurities I had because of my hemangioma.

Ever since I was little, children ridiculed me and called me horrendous names like, "ugly eye," and "big eye". Whenever I would come home from school or camp and Mom would ask me how the other kids treated me, or if I was making friends, I would lie and say everything was fine. I didn't want to hurt her. I was living a lie letting Mom and Dad think I was a well-adjusted child and everything was just fine. I didn't want them to worry about me. I thought it would break them if they knew how the other kids teased and hurt me.

I told Sandy about the time I was seven years old attending that new school in Tarzana in the middle of the semester. I was so shy and afraid of the other kids making fun of me. I was so scared that I was terrified of waiting in line to buy milk. Mom would drop a nickel in my lunch bag every day for milk. Each day, instead of buying milk I would just throw the brown paper bag away with the nickel in it. I carried this guilt with me for years. Sandy said that I wasn't an awful person. I was a child given a challenge and I was forced to be strong at a very young age. I was protecting my parents instead of letting them protect me. I was a child playing the role of a parent to my own parents.

I told Sandy how every night when I was little Mom would look at me and say, "You're beautiful." I never believed her. I thought she was saying that because she loved me and she was my mother. Her love was unconditional. So, it was difficult to believe people when they gave me a compliment or told me I was attractive. I never thought it was sincere. I cried when I admitted all this. Sandy urged me to tell Mom everything. It was important that she know all this. I didn't have the heart to tell her. I still didn't want to hurt her.

Mom and I went to Bullock's to get my suit for the shower altered. Mom was always great with seamstresses since she used to sew herself. She was very detailed and picky. We also bought Kaye her gift and we bought Shari Kahn's little boy a birthday present. We looked everywhere for earrings for Mom's dress with no success. "We got so much accomplished today!" Mom said happily. It was a fun day.

Tera came over with the ceremony music I asked her to bring over. We went over the songs on the piano to see which ones I liked. They were all so beautiful. I played, "Seasons" for Tera. I always dreamed of having it played during my wedding ceremony. Tera thought it sounded very depressing. She felt it sounded too much like "Canon in D" (The theme from "Ordinary People.") Mom always thought it was a pretty song whenever I played it for her. But, Tera almost insisted I not use it.

Matt came over later and we all went out to dinner. Matt asked-me about the song. He also thought it was a depressing song. "You know, you have to consider how the mood is going to be," Matt said to me, "This wedding is going to be very sad; people are going to be very emotional as it is. That song will get people down. Just this one particular time, you should probably think about that."

I still did not think that the song sounded dreary. But, if it bothered Matt and Tera that much, I felt I should consider their feelings. I did not want to make anyone feel more sad than they were, especially Matt and Tera.

After everyone left I played all the songs I was planning to show to Jim Cole this Wednesday. I told Mom to listen from her bedroom. I ran up the stairs and asked how she liked them. She thought they were all beautiful.

May 9, 1990

We met with Jim Cole this evening. We went over every single detail. Jim kept saying, "This is going to be great! You have such a special family." Every time Dad told him one of his ideas Jim would say, "I love it!" He was so enthused. Dad had so many plans for the music and Jim loved all of it. Mom said to Jim, "Make this one count!" Dad looked at her and frowned. I knew what she meant. This would be our last celebration together so Jim better make it an unforgettable one for her; for all of us. Jim said, "Don't worry; it will be a fabulous evening!"

Mom looked very sad.

May 10, 1990

I met Maxine at Bullock's to help her register. It was strange that I was the one who knew what she should register for when Tera had just helped me when I didn't have a clue.

Maxine had to register for four place settings. Formal dairy, formal meat, everyday dairy and everyday meat. She had all her patterns picked out. We grabbed some dinner and went to AEPhi. I was trying to get Maxine into "Twin Peaks" but everyone in the TV room wouldn't keep quiet. Alena and I talked about our weddings. She and Jason were getting married in August. While Alena was talking about all her details all I could think about was how she didn't have any problems.

She was planning her wedding freely and looking forward to it with such excitement. I was jealous. It was supposed to be that way for all brides. I had to think about Mom not becoming more sick and God forbid the possibility of her not even being at the wedding. It was so unfair that I had to worry about these things at a moment that was supposed to be the best time of my life. I had to stop feeling sorry for myself and focus on Mom getting better.

May 11, 1990

Matt and Tera were over for dinner. Mom and Dad told us that they were going to a different doctor for a second opinion. This doctor thought Mom should have this drastic treatment every three weeks. The treatment was so severe that each time she went in she would have to be hospitalized for three days. This was so she could be monitored closely in case her white blood cell count dropped or if her kidneys failed. It would also leave her extremely weak.

There were no guarantees that it would help her any, but this doctor strongly thought she should do it. Dr. Averon was opposed to the whole thing. He thought it wouldn't help her at all and that it would only make Mom feel more sick. But, Mom was willing to try anything to prove to us that she was doing the best she could to fight. If she did decide to go through with it she would have to go in as soon as possible. They were scheduling these treatments around the wedding date so that the treatment she would have before the wedding would give her enough time to recuperate. This seemed like a nightmare.

Mom said to all of us, just as she had said several times before, that she felt she had a full life. She was so proud of us. She had a long, loving marriage, beautiful children, and had no regrets. "I feel real, real lucky," Mom said firmly. "I feel that my life of less than fifty years has been more fruitful than a woman who has lived to be one hundred. Just because I'm not going to live a long time, it doesn't mean that my life hasn't been as fulfilling. I'm very thankful."

She was so brave and grateful. She acted like she wasn't scared. I know how strong she was and how fulfilled she was, but I also knew there was so much more left for her to do and see. Mom and Dad never went to Israel like they had planned. Every time they had plans to go, something with Mom's cancer came up and the doctor would advise her not to go. It was so unfair.

I wanted Mom to see what I saw and come home and share it with me; talk about Israel together. But, this would never happen. The thing that hurt more than anything else was that Mom would never see her grandchildren. What was even more painful was that her grandchildren would never know her. Mom would have been the best Grandma in the world, (second to Grandma Betty, of course.)

She was always so excited over the thought of me having children and she would baby-sit and be a grandma. Mom said that it was so much more special when your daughter gives you a grandchild than when your son does. Mom loved Matt with all her heart and adored and loved Tera like her own. But Mom knew that I would let her do whatever she pleased with my children. Tera would be more fussy, Mom thought.

It broke my heart finding the difficulty in imagining Dad as "Grandpa Nat" without "Grandma Bernice." Although I was planning on telling my children about Mom through stories, photos, and videos I was afraid of that void in my children's lives. Having grown up with all four of my grandparents I felt a strong importance in the value of grandparents. Mine were such a positive influence in my life; I learned so much from them and had the fondest of memories.

And, because Grandma Betty was the only one still alive I knew what it was like to have such a special grandmother. She told me stories and stories and tales and tales; sad ones, funny ones, maybe even phony ones. She was so precious to me. I knew my children would know mom through the values I planned to teach them and the love I would give them, but it didn't ease my pain one bit.

I wanted Mom in their lives. I wanted her in mine.

May 12, 1990

I had a gown fitting today. Mom wanted to go with me so badly but she just didn't have the strength. I really wanted her there with me more than ever before. Before the fitting I had my hair and make-up done to see exactly how I would look with the dress and head piece. When I looked at myself in the mirror it seemed meaningless without Mom there. I needed her to tell me there was a wrinkle in the train, or not enough poof in the sleeve, or the veil was too scarce, or my hair should be up instead of down.

Dianne Taylor and Michelle Bran from A E Phi were there. "Sharon, you look beautiful," Dianne said. I just wish it was Mom saying that. Dianne's wedding was in three weeks. I was so envious of her. Mine was in six weeks, which seemed like an eternity away for Mom. I began to wonder what I would do if G-d forbid, Mom didn't make it. I looked at myself in the mirror again with the dress, headpiece, make-up and hair. Instead of being excited I was sad and empty. I was lonely not sharing this special moment with Mom. And this wasn't even the real thing.

When I got home I asked Mom what she thought of my hair and make-up. She liked it a lot. I wanted her to since she was going to use the same hairdresser and make-up artist. She just didn't have the strength to go in for herself to experiment.

Tom sent me huge personalized Mylar balloons for our three year anniversary. One said, "I Love You Sharon," Another said, "Happy Three Year Anniversary," and the others said, "I Love You," and other mushy things. I dragged them upstairs to show Mom and Dad. Dad was laughing. He always made fun of Tom for being so extravagant. Mom loved them. She told me to put them on display downstairs in the den so everyone could see them. They were so cute.

I admired the collage for Mom, which I finally finished that week. I couldn't wait to see Mom's face tomorrow. It came out as moving as I imagined it would be. I signed it from all of us: Matt, Tera, Sharon, Tom, and Stephen. It was going to be a surprise for everyone. I couldn't wait. The pictures looked beautiful surrounding my poem.

The poem read:

Being your children is a joy and a blessing.

We reflect upon our lives with joyful reminiscing.

When we needed your support you were always there,

With never-ending patience, compassion and care.

Your smile let us know that everything would be okay,

Your sweet words brought our spirits up and helped us through our day.

Your strength taught us to never give up on our dreams.

Your wisdom guided us and enabled us to see.

Your positive outlook on life taught us to never lose hope,

To face the world with confidence and learn how to cope.

Forgiveness always had a special place in your heart,

You helped us learn from our mistakes by granting us a new start.

In our times of need you have always stayed by our side.

You encouraged us to believe in ourselves through your eyes of pride.

You have shown us that you are the most wonderful mother and wife,

Above all, you gave us the precious gift of life.

Happy Mother's Day Mom!

I knew Mom would love it. I hoped the presence of it beside her bed would brighten her days and let her never lose sight of her hope.

Tonight Tom and I went to Tom's cousin, Jordan's Bar Mitzvah. It was a great party but I just couldn't enjoy myself. I was so depressed and I couldn't snap out of it.

May 13, 1990

It was just Mom and I this morning. Dad was golfing and Matt and Stephen were playing softball. We were all meeting for brunch at Matt and Tera's later. Mom and I were at the kitchen table when I wished her a happy Mother's Day. I told her I would be right back. I ran upstairs to get the collage. I was so anxious to give it to her. I had butterflies in my stomach. I said "Happy Mother's Day" as I stood the collage in front of her.

"Oh, my G-d," she said. I watched her face as her eyes wandered over the collage. Her eyes were filled with tears, admiration, and surprise. "It's beautiful," she said crying. I love your little poems." Her eyes roamed up and down again and again. "The pictures are so nice." She especially liked the one of Matt's graduation. "I like that picture because of the tears in my eyes," she said dreamily. "This must have taken you a lot of time... the poem, the framing, the matting..." I wanted Mom to see that making this for her wasn't "time" to me. I got so much joy out of doing it. I wanted her to enjoy it for a long, long time.

I went to Matt and Tera's before Mom and Dad got there. To my surprise Dad had the collage cradled in his arm as they walked in. He showed Matt, Tera and Stephen and said "Look what Sharon made for us." Dad walked over to me and embraced me tightly. He said through sobs, "Sharon, I'm so proud of you. I love you so much. You're so talented. Thank you sweetie. It's so beautiful." His body was shaking with emotion and tears. Although I was so happy Dad was touched by Mom's gift his reaction terrified me. Did he know how much time she had? Was it sooner than I was thinking?

After brunch Mom and I went to the Promenade to look for earrings for her dress. As we walked into Robinson's I got this eerie feeling. I clung to Mom's hand supporting her as I helped her walk. I studied her face. She looked so scared. I tried to put myself in her position but it seemed beyond imaginable. I gazed across the store admiring all the beautiful clothes and accessories that would look lovely on Mom. I thought of her never wearing these things, never being in a store shopping again.

Never being in this beautiful world again, surrounded by beautiful things.

When we got to the jewelry department Mom had to sit down. I ran to get her more water. She was so exhausted yet so determined to find earrings. Robinson's had nothing. Mom got the Clinique gift. That was always fun to do together. New make-up should lift her spirits up. As we walked towards Sak's she said, "Wait, I have to sit down again. I'm sorry." We sat on a bench.

I made a note in my mind to remember the exact location of that bench we sat on together.

I had this feeling we would never go shopping together again. It was too much for Mom. I looked at my surroundings to savor that moment. I thought of it as "the spot in the mall where Mom and I once sat." It was so painful imagining her not in my life. I didn't want mom to see my pain. I had to be strong for her.

When we finally made it to Sak's, Mom was ready to go home. I didn't want Mom walking all the way back to where the car was parked so I walked back to the car and drove to Sak's to pick her up. Poor Mom just didn't have the strength. And to think she won a tennis tournament just a few months ago. It was unbelievable.

May 14, 1990

Tom and I finally decided we would buy that Mario Braundo comforter set we saw at Bullock's. I couldn't believe how Tom was so crazy about it. It was a very Laura Ashley style and so feminine. I was so happy he loved it so much. The whole set was so expensive. Mom surprised us and said that the entire comforter set, including the dust ruffle, shams, sheets and pillows was our shower gift from her. That was so sweet of her and just like her to be so giving like that.

The whole set was delivered to our house in a humungous box. She wanted me to go to Bullock's to get it gift wrapped so I could open it at the shower on Sunday. I thought that was so silly to wrap my own gift. Mom and I just wished things were normal so we wouldn't have to think of such stupid ideas. We decided I would just acknowledge her gift at the shower but it just wasn't the same.

Late that night, Stephen came into my room. It looked like he had been crying. From the doorway he yelled, "Did you know Mom is going to the hospital tomorrow?"

When I said, "Yes, I'm visiting her after work," he looked very steamed.

"How come nobody told me? She's not getting better is she?" I was silent. "Is she!!" he demanded.

I was sitting on my bed. I patted the side next to me to motion him to sit down next to me. By now he couldn't stop crying. His tears were of rage, bitterness, and pain. I didn't want to make him feel worse by saying that the reason he was so oblivious to what was going on was because he was never around and always at the fraternity or with Julia. He just needed to be told the truth. The sad thing was, I wasn't even sure what the truth was.

He talked about his friend Shirley's father dying of cancer. He said that before he died he lost tons of weight and the same thing was happening to Mom. I tried to reason with him that every cancer victim was different, but Stephen was probably right. That was a bad sign.

Stephen's beautiful hazel eyes were blood shot overflowing with tears. He said that he was frustrated because every time he tried to have a conversation with Mom he couldn't because he was being constantly interrupted by Mom's coughing. In between every word Mom spoke came out a horrible cough from the fluid in her lungs, and chest. Mom and Stephen used to always talk and laugh together. He thought it was unfair that Matt and I had her support during college and he was losing her help and support. He was used to her helping him with his papers and cooking for him all the time. He was really Mom's baby. I told him that even though she can't talk to him like they used to because of her coughing, he should still spend time with her.

"But, it's not the kind of time I want to spend with her. I hate looking at her; she doesn't look the same!" Stephen yelled. It hurt a lot to see Mom deteriorate, but to me she was still so beautiful. I urged Stephen to still be with her. Just sitting in the same room with her would be something he could look back upon and remember, and have no regrets. I felt like he was getting a raw deal because he was the youngest and still at an age where he needed Mom so much. Of course, Matt and I needed Mom just as much but in a different way. Stephen had always depended on Mom's help in school and she was his primary motivation to do well and graduate college. I hugged him hard as we both cried. I acted much stronger than I was feeling on the inside. My insides were tearing apart from pain and fear.

May 15, 1990

Mom went to the hospital for her first of her treatments today. She was so scared. She thought the treatment was going to kill her and that she would never come out of the hospital alive. Despite all her fright she was determined to go through with this drastic treatment to see how her body would respond. I wondered how much she was doing this for herself. She was terrified. It seemed like she was going through this torture to show us that she was trying her hardest to fight and was doing everything she could for us. I was so scared for her.

I told her I would visit after work. I went to Robinson's so Nancy could do my make-up with the Chanel line. Since Mom and I were planning on getting our make-up done together by the same person for the wedding I wanted to test Nancy out and show Mom. When I compared the way Charlie did my make-up last Saturday I was so confused. I figured whoever Mom liked more we would go from there.

After Robinson's I went to Cedar-Sinai to see Mom. Hospitals always gave me a creepy feeling. I hated the smell and the icy cold feeling. It gave me goose-bumps. The closer I was getting to Mom's room the more I got chills. I never wanted Mom to die in the hospital so I tried not to imagine it. I wanted her to die at home, in her bed, where she belonged.

I slowly opened the door of Mom's room. She was extremely uncomfortable. Dad looked worn out and miserable. I asked who all the flowers were from. One arrangement was from Sandy and Art and the other was from Jack, our florist. Although they were just beautiful, not even flowers could cheer up Mom's room. It was so dreary in there. It was cloudy outside; Mom kept complaining that she was freezing. It frightened me because Dad and I found the room to be a comfortable temperature. She was bundled up with blankets, but was still very cold.

Mom asked if I had trouble finding her room, where I parked, and if I had a tough time finding her. Although I parked far and it did take me a long time to search for her room (I parked near the wrong tower) I told her I had no problems. Even when she was in pain and was fighting for her life she showed concern for me. She was a true mother, always worried about her children when she had her own misery to deal with.

I asked her how she liked the make-up. She said it looked beautiful. When I asked which make-up job she liked better compared to Saturday's she replied, "I like them both." Mom gave me a huge smile because she knew she was confusing me. She said whoever I decided to use would be fine with her.

I could tell Mom was exhausted and in a lot of discomfort. I had a feeling she would not plan on having this treatment again in three weeks. It just seemed to beat up her body and spirit.

May 16, 1990

Grandma told me that Mom went in for her treatment to prove to us that she tried her best. She did not want to let us down. She was not just fighting for herself. She was fighting to live for us. She felt that if she did the treatment we would think she was not giving up. She wanted us to know she did her best to survive. It was heartbreaking for me to hear this. All that pain, discomfort, and loneliness of a hospital.

Being so exhausted from such a severe treatment. Having foreign chemicals shoot through her body only to beat it up even more. All to prove that she was fighting to the end.

All for her family.

She cared about us so much.

May 17, 1990

The actress Jill Ireland died. It really saddened me. I read every article written on her death. The trades, USA Today, and others. Her attitude and outlook was exactly like Mom's. Being brave, never losing dignity, hope, determination to fight the deadly disease, never losing pride, never being ashamed, afraid. Living life instead of thinking of death. Giving others hope. Always smiling and cheerful. Never complaining about the pain and discomfort.

What was so scary was Jill Ireland's cancer and history of her disease was exactly like Mom's. Diagnosed with breast cancer six years ago. No family history of the disease. Lymph nodes removed. Spread to bones and lungs later on, etc. Even her treatments were the same. The same amount of chemotherapy, radiation, and operations. Exactly like Mom's fight. It was eerie. The only difference was Jill Ireland was older. She died at 54. Mom was only 49. Her life should have been beginning, not ending. It was so unfair.

There was one thing I read that gave me some hope. It was reported that Jill Ireland's last public appearance was at her son's wedding two weeks before her death. I thought of what Rachel and I talked about. Rachel had read that deaths increase following the holidays, which may indicate that many people die right after a significant event. I know it was purely coincidental, but maybe just maybe Jill Ireland lived to see her son's wedding and then her body finally gave in. Maybe the same thing would happen with Mom. What hurt so much was that I wanted so much. I didn't just want Mom at my wedding; I wanted her always.

And I knew I couldn't have that.

May 18, 1990

Matt and Tera came over for dinner. Mom looked very frail. She did not look like herself. Her facial expressions were stiff. When she smiled her mouth smiled halfway. I had never seen her look so ill. I always thought that if a stranger saw her, he or she would never know she had cancer. But, tonight she looked different. She had no appetite and barely ate anything. "I'm going upstairs," Mom said. "I'm real tired."

When Mom got to the top of the stairs, Matt said, "We better move up the wedding."

"When?" I asked.

"As soon as possible," Matt answered. "This weekend."

"Mom is just feeling sick from her treatment," I said defensively. "She will feel much better for the wedding."

"She's getting worse," Matt said. "Look at her. She could barely make it up the stairs. Imagine what she'll be like in a month."

Dad said we would leave the wedding date as it was. He then turned to me and said, "Do you know what's happening?" His hand was on my shoulder. "Are you dealing with this?"

I burst into hysterical tears. Matt started weeping and said under his breath, "She's dying."

I didn't want to believe him, and cried even harder. I kept thinking of how Tom said to always look into Mom's eyes.

They were so clear and white. As long as her eyes were white she just could not be dying. Tom was such an optimist.

Matt asked if Tom knew that Mom might not make it to the wedding. He said he thought Tom was in for a rude awakening.

I asked Dad if he thought she would make it to the wedding. He said there was no telling but there was a good chance she would not make it.

My heart froze and my stomach dropped. We were all crying by now.

I always believed Mom would make it until that moment. I was so ignorant. I never thought of Mom dying so soon. Mom was too strong a fighter. Her spirit would never give in to cancer, I thought. And now it looked like I was wrong. Because of my own innocence I was wrong the whole time.

Tom just got in from work. He had been waiting outside looking through the door. He didn't want to walk in at the wrong time. He sat beside me and started crying. Tom's hopes were let down probably more than mine. He was the optimistic one throughout Mom's whole battle. I was always telling him to wake up and face reality. But, he was so stubbornly positive. He always emphasized that Mom was a fighter. There was no doubt in Tom's mind that Mom was going to win her battle. When Tom finally convinced me that Mom would make it and I believed in his high hopes it hit me in the face hard and I was mad at myself for believing him.

Before I met Tom I had a philosophy that if you didn't expect things you would never get let down. Tom thought that was having a pessimistic outlook on life. He always took a positive approach. I tried his way. I hoped, and prayed, and told myself that Mom was a survivor and that she had such a strong will to be at the wedding that there was no way she would die. I believed all those stories of cancer victims using their positive emotions; the mind over body theory.

But, Mom was always positive. She read books, used visual imagery, concentrated on life, not death. She wanted more than anything to live and become healthy again. She always had high spirits and said out loud many times, "I've just got to fight this!" And here we were. I was optimistic and was let down. I hurt myself by being hopeful. I felt like a fool.

I always loved Mom with all my heart and knew how much I needed her. But, at that moment I wanted her to be a part of my life more than ever before. It hurt so much. We all just kept on crying.

Dad said he bought the house for Mom. Dad said Mom was supposed to be the "rich widow." Mom and Dad did not plan on things to work out this way. Dad always expected that Mom would outlive him. Dad said softly beneath the sound of his sobs, "so much to look forward to and now it's all meaningless. I envy those who will celebrate their 50th anniversary. I always imagined Mom and I having a big 50th anniversary with all our grandchildren. My life has been so blessed. I guess something bad just had to happen to balance it out. Life is a scale. You have a series of wonderful events and then a tragedy hits you. It had to happen. My life was so perfect."

I asked how Mom felt; if she was afraid. Dad said she wasn't afraid of dying. She was only afraid of the pain. "She's had it," Dad said. "When she was in the hospital for the drastic treatment she thought she wouldn't come out alive. She's ready to go. There's too much pain... she's no longer living. This is no way to live."

Terri asked if Dad would consider getting a nurse for Mom. "No," Dad answered abruptly as if he had already thought about it. "I'm not ready for that."

You know, everybody wants to help to show they care. When you love someone you get satisfaction out of helping them. It really showed the past few months. The phone rang off the hook every hour, friends were offering to bring dinner over each night, and of course we were so grateful for Kaye. Thank G-d for Kaye. She was Dad's lifesaver. She was doing everything she could to help out and take care of Mom. Dad went on to say, "I feel good when I take care of her myself. I'm not ready for a nurse yet."

Tera said she knew someone for when Dad was ready. I told everybody that Stephen needed to be spoken to. He never knew what was happening. They all said he was never around but we knew that wasn't the point. "We have to be there for each other," Dad said. I told Dad that Stephen and I had a long talk the other night. "That's good," he said. "It's important."

Dad urged us that if we had anything we wanted to tell Mom we ought to tell her soon. "I don't want you to have any regrets" he sobbed. "I think about my father all the time. I miss him so much. All my life, no matter what was happening, I knew he loved me."

I missed Grandpa Joe so much. He was the first person I knew and loved to have died. I never thought he would die when he had cancer. Just like Mom. Dad was crying even harder. Dad seemed to address what he was going to say next to me. "Even when you and Mom had your differences she always loved you... she always cared."

I knew that. I had to let Mom know I knew that. There were so many things I never told Mom. So many secrets I had been keeping inside since I was a little girl. I was afraid that if I told Mom all these things she would know I was telling her everything because I was admitting that she was dying. I didn't want her thinking I had lost hope.

I cried all night.

May 20, 1990

Today was my bridal shower at Val's. While I was getting ready I was so nervous and so worried about Mom. I had to rush to get Mom ready and myself on time. I was so afraid I would forget something. I had Mom's oxygen tank, Kaye's gift, but I felt so stressed, as if I was forgetting something. I was rushing around the house with my head somewhere else. I was unbelievably nervous. Instead of being excited I was angry that I was so depressed. Mom said, "You're being a grouch. You better act pleasant today." Later, in the car she said she was sorry. "I know it's real hard but you have to try and not be grouchy and be up."

Kaye really went all out with her classy style. The room and decor was just beautiful and the food was delicious. The place was so elegant. Mom looked so pretty and radiant in her black and white suit. I didn't even think she looked ill. To me, she looked healthy. Everyone was crowding around Mom. They were so happy to see her. She got so many compliments. She never stopped smiling. She was wagging her cane as she sat down and socialized with everyone.

When Mom left our table for a minute Tom's grandmother Jan snapped at me, "She hasn't lost that much weight!"

Sandy said, "Mom, she has lost a lot."

Jan shouted back, "She doesn't look that bad! I still don't know why she didn't have a mastectomy. I had one and I'm fine!"

I tried to remain calm. This was my bridal shower and I was going to act like a lady. I explained to Jan nicely when she had cancer it was fifteen years ago and things were different now. Mom had more options. She had radiation, chemotherapy and her lymph nodes removed instead of a mastectomy.

She yelled, "So did I! How many lymph nodes did she have removed?"

I wasn't sure, but I replied, "Six."

Jan screamed, "I had fourteen and Jill Ireland only had ten removed! And she just died!"

I wanted to scream but I wasn't going to make a scene at my own shower. I wouldn't have said anything even if it wasn't my shower. It was no use. How dare she say what my Mom should have done well after the fact.

Jan acted like some hero because she beat cancer and my mom was still fighting. What a ruthless manner she had. Sandy was still explaining everything to her and putting her in her place. Tamara was trying to hear what we were talking about. I told her "never mind."

Even though I was infuriated I wanted to have a pleasant day. Mom was there and that was what mattered.

Tamara kept saying, "Your next shower is only two weeks away! Before you know it, after that the wedding will be only three weeks away! Time will fly by so fast! Aren't you excited?" I was more anxious and antsy than excited. I felt like the clock was ticking away slowly and that June 24 was eons away. It seemed like an eternity away at that time. G-d only knew what kind of condition Mom would be in by then. I tried to enjoy myself as best as I could.

When Tom and Dad walked in everyone cheered. My two favorite men, I thought to myself.

For every gift I opened I looked at Mom to see her reaction. She looked so happy and excited for me. Her face was shining with pride and love for me. I was so happy she was there.

She made me so proud. It was a magnificent day.

May 21, 1990

When I got home from work I sat with Mom at the kitchen table. She said, "I've been getting endless calls today from people saying how beautiful you were yesterday. How you were so poised, eloquent, appreciative and cheerful. They went on and on about how you are going to make a lovely bride. I'm very, very, very, proud of you." Her pride showed in her face.

It meant so much to me to hear that from Mom. Making Mom proud was the world to me. I guess it goes way back to the times when I wanted her approval so desperately. I always knew she was proud of me but to hear those words from her made me so happy.

Tom slept over. In the middle of the night he heard me crying and woke up and held me. He was crying too. "Sharon I'm so worried about you. You've got to tell her soon, you've just got to tell her everything before it's too late. I'm worried for you. You'll never forgive yourself. Please talk to her soon." Tom couldn't stop crying. "Promise me you'll talk to her." I promised him. I just didn't know when.

May 22, 1990

Each evening I drove home from work I always got an insecure feeling of Mom not being alive when I walked in the door. It was such a helpless feeling that I had no control over. I was so happy to see her lying in her bed.

"Hi, sweetie," Mom said lovingly with a big smile. I laid down on Dad's side of the bed and we talked for a while. She confided in me which made me feel so good. She said like an innocent little child, "I've had such a good life that I'm thankful for but I feel ungrateful for all the good things I've had because I still want to live. I'm bummed about all the good things I'm going to miss. But, I don't want that to seem like I'm not thankful for what I've had in my life. I have so many wonderful things to look forward to and I'm going to miss them. It's not fair. But, I don't want anyone to think that I'm not thankful."

I told her it was okay to feel that way. We knew how appreciative she was of her blessings. And, at the same time she had the right to live just like anybody else. This was supposed to be the best year of Mom's life. If Mom was healthy we would have given her a huge surprise party for her 50th birthday this June 13th. Then Mom and Dad's 30th Anniversary was coming this June 26th. And of course Mom was so excited for her only daughter's wedding and we were expecting Tera to become pregnant any day so Mom would have her first grandchild.

So many wonderful things. It was so unfair. Mom and Dad had so many beautiful things to look forward to and Mom wouldn't be here and Dad would not have Mom to share these things with. But, at the same time Mom was such a decent woman that in spite of the bad hand she was dealt she was worried that her will to live would appear as if she was ungrateful for her wonderful life.

I did not understand why a person like Mom had to suffer like this when there were too many people in this world who go on living and don't even take the time to count one blessing.

Mom once said how much she hated the sport, boxing. "Here are these people trying to kill each other while I am laying here struggling to stay alive." She was so right. Mom was fighting this battle between living and dying while millions of people were taking their lives for granted. Life was truly a gift. Mom loved hers so much... she just wanted more of it.

We all did.

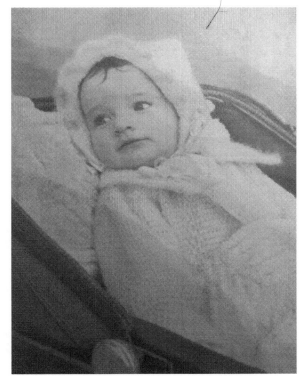

Bernice Berlant (my mommy), June, 1940, Brooklyn NY

My parents, teenage lovebirds, 1956, NY

Mom and Dad's wedding, June 26, 1960

Mommy and me, 1966

May, 1983, a year before my Mom's diagnosis

August, 1984, one month after diagnosis. My mom knitted the sweater she's wearing

My graduation from UCLA, June 1988

June 25, 1989, one year before my Mom's passing

February, 1990, four months prior to my Mom's passing

May 20, 1990, at my bridal shower. My Mom passed just 18 days later

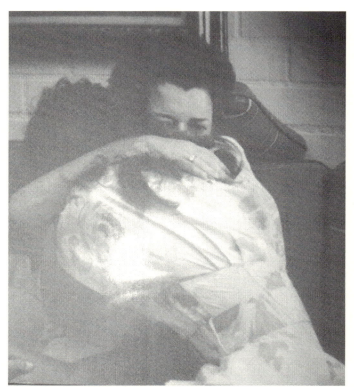
June 3, 1990 at my 2nd bridal shower. This was our last hug. My Mom passed four days later

May 23, 1990

Tom slept over last night. He always slept on the floor next to my bed, but early this morning he got into bed with me just for one second. It was around 6:00 in the morning. Dad opened my door without knocking and I screamed from the shock. I thought my worst nightmare was reality. "What's wrong?" I screamed. I feared that Mom just died.

"Relax," Dad said. "Your car has a flat tire. Here are Mom's keys; take her car to work this morning. I'm leaving to golf now."

I never felt such relief in my life. Dad startled me over nothing. The funny thing was he probably thought I screamed because he found Tom in my bed when he should have been on the floor. The one time Tom innocently got into bed with me, Dad had to walk in. Tom kept saying he didn't even look phased. I was still trying to catch my breath from that shock. Thank G-d Mom was still alive. My biggest fear was waking in the morning to Dad's scream from finding Mom dead.

I just had to be right next to her when her time came.

When I tried to get the key into the ignition of Mom's car I was struggling with it. I must have tried for about ten minutes. As much as I hated myself for doing this I went inside to ask Mom for help. To my surprise she came outside in her nightgown and struggled with the key. It just wasn't working. I tried turning the wheel and it still wouldn't work. Mom was very frustrated. I felt so guilty that she was doing this for me in the hot sun, in a warm car.

She was so determined to get the key to work. She came to the conclusion that they were the wrong keys. We searched everywhere, in every purse.

I didn't want Mom over-exerting herself but there was no stopping her. We found a different set of keys but those didn't work either. I had no choice but to call the Auto Club. I got poor Mom out of bed for this stupidity. Although she was real tired she wasn't going to go back to sleep. We sat at the kitchen table while we waited for the guy to arrive. Just sitting together felt so nice. It was almost as if the key didn't work just so I could spend that morning with Mom.

When the guy got there he tilted the steering wheel and the car started no problem. I felt like an idiot. The guy said I just didn't have the strength and not to feel stupid. The whole way to work I thought of how thankful I was that this happened. I felt so awful that Mom would do anything in the world for me no matter how sick she felt. But it felt good too because we spent some precious time together.

May 24, 1990

Mom and I talked about when Tom and I would start moving stuff into the apartment. We hadn't done anything yet. I was kind of putting it off. I told Mom and Dad half-joking and half-serious that I wanted to stay and live with them.

Mom said, "Okay, that's fine with me! Is that okay, Nat?"

Dad said, "Are you kidding? I thought we were getting rid of you."

I laughed. But, deep inside I wanted to stay until Mom died. I did not want to be living somewhere else and have to face getting a call saying she was gone. I wanted to be there.

When I told Caren that I wanted to live at home after Tom and I were married, she said, "No, you don't. You'll start your new life in your new apartment and it will be fine. It will be good for you to live away from her. You'll appreciate her more."

I told Caren that appreciating my mother wasn't the problem. I did appreciate her. I wasn't taking her for granted. Caren said she knew.

May 25, 1990

Mom and Dad went away for Memorial Day weekend. Dad had a golf tournament in Pebble Beach. I was so excited Mom was able to go somewhere for a whole weekend. I took that as a good sign. Tom was happy about it too.

May 26, 1990

Sandy and I had a very long talk. She said," I want you to know that I will be here for you. I can never be your mommy."

Tears were in her eyes. "No one can ever replace your mommy. But, I love you and I will always care for you."

I wanted to cry but I couldn't. I had this feeling that Sandy promised Mom she would take care of me. I felt so loved by her but I just couldn't embrace that love. At least not at that time. I felt guilty because Sandy wanted to be there for me and I wasn't really welcoming her into my heart like I wanted to. I guess it would just take time.

Fortunately, Sandy understood and her feelings were not hurt.

May 27, 1990

Even though Tom was sleeping over I felt so scared. I told Tom I didn't want to move out after we were married. He looked at me with seriousness and said, "You mean you want to stay here until your Mom dies?"

I started crying and said, "Yes."

Tom nodded his head, held me and said, "Okay, honey, okay we'll stay here. It's okay."

May 28, 1990

Mom was thoroughly exhausted when they got back late this afternoon. I asked if she had a good time, but she said most of the time she was uncomfortable and weak. I guess it was a bad idea for Mom to go along with Dad. But, they NEVER went anywhere without each other. Mom looked worse than when she left. Her complexion was dull and colorless. Her skin was dry and scaly. I noticed her eyes were yellowish.

I thought of what Tom said months ago whenever I cried to him about the possibility of Mom dying. He would always comfort me and say, "Don't worry honey, your Mom's a fighter... I can see it in her eyes... no one with eyes as bright and clear and white as your Mom's could be near death... I just know she is going to make it. Just look into her eyes."

Mom's beautiful blue eyes were now a dreary, gray, and yellow. What was wrong? I asked Dad and he said it was jaundice. The cancer was affecting her liver now. My worst nightmare was coming true. How could anyone survive liver cancer?

I was terrified.

May 30, 1990

Mom and Dad were going to Grandma's after the doctor. I met them at Grandma's after work. All three of them looked miserable. "What did the doctor say?" I asked.

"Not good," was all they replied. Nobody even looked at me. It was as if I wasn't there. Grandma couldn't look at Mom without crying. Mom and Dad looked miserable too. Mom was so much weaker than usual. I walked Mom down Grandma's stairs, which seemed to take forever. Grandma watched us from the top of the stairs sighing in between sobs.

May 31, 1990

The shower being given to me by Tamara and Mandy was this Sunday. Mom decided we should invite Grandma. Grandma told me she just couldn't because she wasn't feeling good from her blood pressure. Mom told me to tell Grandma that she really wanted see her at the shower because she couldn't come to her apartment anymore. It was too difficult to climb all those stairs for Mom.

I called Grandma again and she said, "I'm sorry darling. It breaks my heart to see Mommy so sick. I want to wait until she's better."

I gave the phone to Mom even though I said I wouldn't do it. Mom said, "Please come on Sunday. I want to see you."

I guess Grandma said yes because Mom hung up. It seemed like Mom thought she would never see Grandma again if she didn't see her Sunday.

It frightened me.

That night I went into Mom and Dad's room to finally tell Mom "everything." They were lying in bed and I sat in between them facing them. Mom's head was lying on her pillow with her eyes resting and Dad was sitting up on his pillow.

I said, "I have to talk to you."

Mom could tell what this talk was about. She didn't look the least bit surprised. I think she was expecting this and she probably thought, "Finally."

My voice was shaky as I said, "I have a lot of things I have been keeping inside that I think you should know about."

Mom said, "Uh-oh." Dad looked at me very seriously.

I went on to say, "I have been living a lie. My childhood isn't what I let you think it was."

Dad looked very scared. He held my knee as I spoke. "When I was real little I was very self-conscious of my eye. I was always made fun of and was scared of other children. They called me all kinds of names and I spent a lot of recesses and lunches sitting alone."

I told them how shy it made me and how insecure I was about my appearance. I explained how I thought I would never have a boyfriend. I told them the entire story of when I was seven, in the first grade at the new school in Tarzana where I threw away a nickel every single day because I was too shy to stand in line to buy milk. I knew Mom would make a crack about that. We both figured out how much money I had thrown out and how much it was worth today.

Mom with her cute sense of humor said she wanted the interest. I explained how I thought that if I told them everything was fine they wouldn't worry about me because I could see as a little child how concerned they were for me. I told them that I never turned to them because I didn't want to hurt them. But, I could see in Dad's eyes how hurt he was now.

He said, "I feel terrible that you didn't come to us. We could have done something. We could have talked to your school and teachers or taken you to a counselor. That's what we were there for. I feel awful that you went through that all alone. You sure fooled me. I never knew all this. You seemed so well-adjusted and happy. You were in drama, choir, you had lots of friends, always involved in school and activities. You didn't seem shy at all."

Mom said, "I never knew. I had no idea. You never told us. You seemed to be doing beautifully. We never wanted to treat you differently. We were never ashamed of you. We took you to the beach, the zoo, the park, everywhere. We were so proud of how well you adjusted. I had no idea."

I told them that although I turned out okay, my early childhood memories left scars. I still had deep insecurities about my looks.

Both Mom and Dad said at the same time, "But, you turned out to be beautiful. We are very lucky you came out of this so beautifully."

Dad said with relief, "Thank G-d you came out okay. You scared me·. I thought you were going to say that you were molested or something."

I felt awful that Dad thought that even for one minute. I guess I did set it up to sound like that was what I was going to tell them. Dad said that I should never have lied. He wondered what they did wrong to make me not want to come to them. That's what parents are for. He felt terrible that I wanted to protect them when they could have been protecting me.

Mom was very quiet and tired.

Dad and I ended up talking for a very long time in great detail. This talk turned out to be for Mom and Dad, not just Mom. Dad joked, "Is there anything else you want to tell us?"

Stephen came in and asked what was going on. Dad said, "Sharon has just confessed to us all her dark secrets."

Stephen asked what it was all about. I told him I was adopted. We all laughed.

I didn't feel any sense of relief from this talk. I felt terrible for hurting Dad. I wasn't sure if it really served any purpose in telling them all those things after all.

June 1, 1990

Mom's condition was worsening before our eyes. She was deteriorating rapidly more and more each day. Tera said she spoke to Dr. Averon. I was surprised he took her call. She said they released the confidentiality and any of us could call and the doctor would speak to us.

I asked Tera if Dr. Averon thought Mom would make it to the wedding. Tera said Dr. Averon said Mom had about three to four weeks. I could feel my insides turning. I felt hot flashes and chills all at once. I was too shocked to cry. I was uncomfortably numb.

The wedding was three weeks and two days away. Even if Mom was still alive I cringed at the sight of her in three weeks. I didn't want to humiliate her in front of 230 people. Only G-d could foresee the condition Mom would be in. Would she even be coherent in three weeks? How could this be happening? Mom planned the entire wedding.

Mom's voice was going through my head. All those millions of times she said in desperation, "Oh, I've GOT to make it... I've got to be there" she would always say with determination and hope, her voice trembling with fear of the unknown. And now I looked at her and she was surrendering. Who could blame her? She was in so much pain and could no longer enjoy her life, bedridden, never knowing if she would wake up alive the next morning. What kind of way was that to live?

Kaye, Tera, and I were planning on taking Mom for her final dress fitting tomorrow. Matt and Tera realized how impossible it was going to be for Mom to go. She was running out of strength. Tera said she knew a medical center where we could buy a wheelchair on short notice. What a great idea! We didn't want to tell Mom we were doing it. We were afraid she wouldn't like the idea. Matt and Stephen were going to pick it up in the morning before we left for Mom's dress fitting.

Dad asked me if I could take care of Mom tomorrow. He was leaving the house around 7:00 a.m. so he wanted me to give Mom her medication at 8:00 a.m., 12:00, etc.

Before I went to sleep I sat with Mom for a while. Mom said timidly, "You know, I haven't washed my hair in a week."

It was too difficult for Mom to stand in the shower and too painful for her for me to wash her hair in the sink. "I still have my dignity," Mom whimpered.

She wanted to look nice for her dress fitting and just in general. I told her I would give her a sponge bath tomorrow morning. Her face lit up like a little kids. She agreed it was a nice idea.

June 2, 1990

When I went into Mom's room to give her her medication she was sitting up, wide awake. "Good morning, sweetie. Are you going to take care of me today?" she said with a warm smile.

We went downstairs to the kitchen for breakfast. Mom wasn't hungry at all. I asked what she felt like having. She said she just wanted cookies. She could tell by the expression on my face that only having cookies had no nutritional value.

She admitted, "I know that's terrible, but that's all I want for now."

She barely ate one cookie and had a half a sip of milk. I decided to have her drink one of those "Ensure" drinks. She thought that was a great idea. She suddenly became excited over it. But, she barely drank half of it.

"You have to eat something to survive," I told her.

"I know" Mom cried in a frightened little girl voice. I didn't mean to scare her.

"I didn't mean it that way" I told her. "You need your strength."

As I was helping Mom up the stairs I noticed Matt and Stephen pulling up the driveway. They were setting up the wheelchair they just picked up.

"What's going on out there?" she asked curiously. "Nothing," I answered.

I felt so silly saying that. I could never fool Mom. But, we were all so uncertain over her reaction to this wheelchair business.

"Something's going on out there" she said.

I walked Mom up the stairs. A few minutes later Matt and Stephen came up.

"We have a surprise for you," Matt said enthusiastically. Mom looked excited. "Oh, goodie! What is it?" she asked.

We walked her down the stairs and waiting for her at the bottom of the staircase was the wheelchair. "Oh, dear" Mom said.

We told her we thought it would make today easier for her since she was going for her dress.

"That was thoughtful of you. Thank you," she said graciously.

We helped her in the wheelchair. When Stephen moved her around she said, "This is fun!" It was just like Mom to make a situation that was hard to deal with a positive experience. Her original sense of humor and her pride and optimism kept her dignified and never allowed her to feel humility. I was so proud of her strength and high spirits. I was looking at a person who loved life so much. It hurt that this person was my mother and that sometime soon I would have to let go and so would she.

I was so nervous about giving Mom a sponge bath. We weren't sure how we were going to do this because Mom wanted me to wash her hair too. She wanted to try and take a shower.

Standing for that long was so difficult for her. I helped her sit on the little bench in the shower. Mom was so embarrassed even though I was making her feel as comfortable as possible. It was very awkward. She was so determined to have me give her this shower. As I washed her body, I found her skin to be unbelievably dry. It was as if her skin had no life.

Mom was concerned because I was getting all wet while I was standing in the shower. She amazed me. All I wanted was for her to feel fresh and clean to keep up her dignity and she felt guilty that I was getting wet in the process.

She was so cute. After I dried her off she said, "Thank you. That wasn't so bad."

I did her hair and make-up. Her hair fell out in patches with each stroke of the brush. This wasn't new to either of us, but it didn't mean it wasn't painful to see. Mom's skin just would not take the make-up. It had lost all its moisture and was so dry. She could barely open her eyes for the eye make-up. Her eyes had lost all their rich blue color. They were yellow-gray and lifeless. Her eye-lashes had fallen off, and her eye-lids were desperate for moisture.

I tried my very best with the make-up. She was still so beautiful to me. I never thought she needed make-up to enhance her beauty. She was so naturally beautiful. I just wanted her to feel good about herself.

Mom wanted me to pick out an outfit for her. It brought back fond memories of when I was real little during kindergarten and first grade. During breakfast I would ask Mom what I was going to wear that day. She would surprise me every morning by having my outfit on my bed. It was usually a dress or a jumper. Now it was my turn to pick out Mom's outfit and to dress her.

I began to feel the role reversal. Mom was always the one who bathed me, washed my hair, styled it, helped me go the bathroom, fed me, and dressed me. Now, I was doing all these things for her.

At that realization, Dad's words of wisdom became so clear to me. I once asked Dad about the song, "You Needed Me." I thought it should have been called, "I Needed You." Dad said there was a special feeling of being needed by someone.

"It feels much better to feel needed than to need someone. Nothing feels better than being needed by someone" he said.

He was so right. Mom needed me and I felt so good. I needed her and it hurt because she couldn't be there for me like she had been all my life. I loved the feeling of this role reversal. I was able to understand the fulfillment that Mom felt out of raising and nurturing me. My mother was teaching me how to be a mother by letting me take care of her. It also reminded me of how much I was going to need Mom when I would have my own children. It was very difficult to accept. I couldn't imagine having babies without Mom on the other end of the phone line telling me what to do next.

I asked her once, "How do you know how to take care of a baby?"

She put it so simply. "You just pick it up and love it." And that was exactly what she did.

Kaye and Tera came over to go to Nicole's for Mom's dress. We managed very well with the wheelchair. I made sure I had Mom's medication for noon, her water bottle, and shoes and earrings to try on with her dress. When we got there Mom was very weak. It took a while helping her into the boutique. I kept wondering how she would manage at the wedding being in the shape she was in.

I was worried for her.

The saleswomen in the shop cheerfully greeted us. They were always so pleasant and excited to see Mom. If they only knew.

Mom tried on the dress. She had a lot of difficulty slipping on her shoes because her feet had been swelling. She started to cry. She later told me why she cried.

She said, "The most simple things, I can't even do anymore. Before, I could just slip on my shoes without a problem. When I couldn't get them on I just got emotional."

I felt awful for Mom. Once she had the dress on, the shoes on, and the earrings, she studied herself in the mirror. She looked ravaged. Her eyes were bulging. She had this sad look on her face. The way I read the expression on her face was frightening. It was, "I am never going to wear this dress, I am not going to make it to the wedding, so I will not be able to wear this dress; I want to but I just know I won't."

She looked confused and scared. She sat down and said, "I'm a mess."

"You're not a mess!" Kaye said to Mom. Mom was looking down. She could barely keep her head up. It was just terrible. I felt helpless. I also felt guilty for putting Mom through all this. Everyone kept telling me not to feel bad. This is what Mom wanted. She was living for my wedding. It was keeping her going. But, when I looked at how hard she was trying it made me feel awful. She was so worried about letting me down.

I know she wanted to be there for herself, but even more for all of us. She was trying with all the strength she had left in her weak, fragile body. The dress did not look the same on her. She had lost a lot of weight since her last fitting. Her body was shaped differently. The gown was so exquisite and had such a life of its own that it made Mom's face look dull and lifeless. So different compared with her last fitting only a month ago. That expression on her face continued to haunt me. I knew it would stay with me forever. I would never forget it.

It scared me so much.

Dad asked me how today went. I told him it went fine. He hugged me and said softly, "Thank you for taking care of her today. I'll need you to do the same for me tomorrow."

I was thrilled to take care of Mom tomorrow. I felt so close to her. Dad was concerned about Mom going to my shower tomorrow. Be didn't think it was a very good idea. He was worried that I would have a hard time handling her and that she wouldn't have the strength being there for a full day. Mom insisted on going.

Later, when Mom and I were alone she asked me, "Don't you think that if I don't go to the shower tomorrow, that that's not living? I mean, don't you think that if I stayed home and laid in bed instead that it's just like not living?"

I totally agreed with her. I was glad she felt that way. She wanted to enjoy what she could. She felt she still had a life that needed to be lived. She went on to say, "I need to be with people. If I go tomorrow, Eileen and Burt will be there to take care of me. They won't let me die. Sandy and Grandma will take care of me. And you'll be there and your friends will be there. You won't let me die, right?"

My heart was breaking into a million pieces. She was beginning to sound like a frightened child. She was terrified of being alone. She felt that if she continued to live and be with people who loved her, she wouldn't die. That explains why all day while she tried to rest she made me lay next to her to make sure she was breathing.

Every time she closed her eyes, she said to me, "Make sure I'm breathing Sharon. Am I breathing? Okay, you'll make sure I'm breathing, okay?"

This happened seconds after she would close her eyes to go to sleep. She was afraid to sleep. She was probably afraid that if she fell asleep she would never wake up. What a way to live. Every time she closed her eyes she abruptly opened them again seconds later. She was so scared of tomorrow. She never knew when her last day would be. I just cried all evening.

Dad said he would come by the shower around 2:00 to check on Mom and would drive her home so she could leave early. He was so worried about me taking care of her tomorrow. But, nothing would stop Mom from being at this shower.

June 3, 1990

At 7:45 this morning, I ran into Mom's room to wake her for her 8:00 medication. But there she was wide awake as can be with Stephen lying in bed next to her.

"Good morning, dear," Mom smiled.

Stephen had already helped her with her medication. I had a feeling that Mom hadn't slept a wink. I walked Mom downstairs to give her some breakfast. Of course she had no appetite. I gave her a glass of "Ensure." That was the only thing she could swallow. She drank half of it. She said she was tired and wanted to lay down upstairs. I thought she should take a nap. The shower wasn't until 12:00 so we had a few hours until we had to start getting ready.

Mom was trying to sleep. I was lying in bed with her on Dad's side. Stephen came in and sat on the floor beside the bed. He was whispering, "I have to go play softball; will you be okay with Mom? How are you going to get yourself ready for the shower and get Mom ready at the same time?"

I told him I would manage, although I was doubting myself. It was going to be tough. We were talking very softly. We didn't want Mom to hear us. Mom said, "Turn up the volume."

I laughed, but Stephen looked concerned.

"No, I'm serious," Mom said. "I can't hear you, turn up the volume."

Stephen said Mom had been saying strange things like that which didn't make sense. He thought she was going crazy. I told him the cancer could be affecting her brain. Or, since her liver wasn't functioning properly her blood was dirty and that could cause swelling of her brain. These thoughts disturbed me. We knew it wasn't the drugs because her dosage hadn't changed at all for several months.

I had to help Mom go to the bathroom very frequently. Even in the bathroom she was afraid to be left alone. She kept calling out my name to make sure I was still there.

Mom just couldn't sleep. She wanted me to lie close to her so I could listen to her breath. She kept saying, "Make sure I'm breathing, okay Sharon?"

Then she would open her eyes to make sure she was still alive. It was so painful to watch her terrified of just taking a nap, fearing death would take her before awakening. It broke my heart to see her so afraid. I felt helpless lying next to her. But, she really wanted me there to make sure she was breathing. I got up to go to the bathroom.

"Where are you going!?" Mom cried. I told her I was just going to the bathroom. "Don't leave me!" she said in a frightened voice.

I went real fast and laid down next to her right away. If the bed shook a little she would ask where I was going. She was so afraid of me leaving the room.

It was time to get ready. I told Mom I was going to take a shower. She begged me to take it in her bathroom so I would be close by. She wanted me to get dressed and ready as close to her as possible even though my bedroom was right next to hers. She was so scared. I felt that she thought that if I left her alone she would die. She probably felt like I was protecting her.

I never felt so happy, sad, and frightened at the same time. It felt so good knowing that she needed me so much. But, at the same time it hurt so much knowing that I was losing her. What scared me the most was that I didn't know when. It seemed like she was going to die on me any minute.

Tera's voice kept ringing through my head and just wouldn't go away: "Dr. Averon said she has about 3 to 4 weeks..."

The wedding was exactly three weeks away and I wasn't even certain if Mom would make it through my shower. I kept telling myself she was strong and she would live through the month. She just had to. She had the will to live so that should be enough I told myself. I was beginning to lose all my hope. At the time that should have been the happiest time in my life all I wanted to do was cry my eyes out.   .

While I was in the bathroom getting ready I would yell to Mom every few moments that I was there. She was so worried that she was alone. This time helping her get ready was even more difficult. I didn't even bother with her make-up because it just would not stay on. Mom could barely open her eyes when I tried to put on her mascara. I tried styling her hair but her hair that was once so thick, shiny, and beautiful was now brittle and falling out in patches. I felt it was too delicate to touch so I just brushed it a little.

I put Mom's jewelry on. Even that was a challenge. I fought and struggled to put on her earrings but the skin of her ear lobes was so dry that her pierced ear holes would not take the earrings. Mom did not want to give up. I just couldn't get them in. I put them in her purse and told her I would try again later.

Even though there was disease inside her she still wanted to look pretty on the outside. But, the dreadful disease had finally caught up with her beauty. To me, she was still beautiful but when she looked at herself she was not satisfied. She finally said, "Who cares." She was thankful that she was going to her daughter's shower.

That's what was important...

Mom was real quiet in the car. She was so exhausted. I was so worried for her. I could not believe this day had finally come. I remember Tamara and Mandy planning the shower months ago. Maxine wanted to help and Caren wanted to help but Tamara just wanted their money, which they didn't have.

The whole thing was driving Mom so crazy that she ended up offering to pay for the shower which Tamara refused. What an unnecessary strain for Mom to go through. And here we were on our way to this shower and Mom was feeling weaker than ever.

When I pulled my car up to Tamara's house, Tamara and Mandy ran out of the house to my car. They must have been looking out the window waiting for us. Burt came out too. When I asked him for help with Mom's wheelchair he looked flabbergasted. "What!?!?" Burt exclaimed. "When did this all happen?"

The last time Burt and Eileen saw Mom was at the shower at Val's just two weeks ago. Mom looked wonderful and was walking around just fine. I guess since I had been seeing Mom every day I didn't see her drastic change as dramatically as Burt and Eileen did. They looked so sad and surprised when they saw Mom. It really disturbed them. They weren't expecting this. Burt helped me set up Mom's wheelchair. Mandy and Tamara and I helped Mom into the wheelchair. We were having so much trouble.

Leanne ran out and kept yelling in her shrieking voice, "I know how to do this, my dad uses a wheelchair!"

We were struggling getting Mom up the stairs to the door. Sandy came out and helped too. This was so much commotion for Mom. She felt that she was so much trouble and felt awful about it. As we were trying to get Mom up the stairs with little success, Mom began to cry.

Sandy put her face real close to Mom's and looked her in the eyes and said firmly, "Bernice, we will get you in, don't worry," and kissed her gently.

Mom just nodded a little. It was a disaster. I did not expect this to be such a scene. It didn't bother me because I was thankful that everyone was so helpful and caring. But I knew Mom did not like all the attention.

Grandma was already there because Sandy drove her. She could barely look at Mom without crying. I didn't see Grandma smile once that whole day. I couldn't blame her.

When we finally got Mom in Tamara's house Tamara, Mandy and Eileen were waiting on Mom hand and foot. I made sure Mom had enough water and felt comfortable.

I kept reminding Mom that if she felt like it she could lay down on a bed in any of the bedrooms. But, she didn't want to miss anything. Burt kept saying, "I don't believe this! This happened so fast!"

Eileen kept asking Mom if she needed anything. She looked so upset at the sight of Mom. I knew how she felt. Sandy tried to cheer Mom up by making a joke out of it. She said to Mom, "Well Bernice, you knew you'd always have this eventually; all these ladies waiting on you like you're the queen." Mom had such a wonderful sense of humor that she was able to giggle a little.

I couldn't even enjoy myself. Instead of greeting all my friends as they arrived, I kept running back and forth to Mom to make sure she was okay. I couldn't keep my eye off of her. I was so preoccupied with Mom that I couldn't enjoy my own shower. But, it just didn't seem important. Mom was the only one that mattered. All my friends greeted Mom with kisses, but I don't even think Mom recognized them. She was so out of it. By the time everyone was there, Mom was my only concern. She kept telling me not to worry about her and be a good hostess. But I just couldn't. Instead, I put on my fake happy face and tried to make the most out of this day that was supposed to be so fun and joyous.

Mom didn't want anything to eat but I fixed her a plate anyway. She barely touched it. Grandma sat with her and frowned the whole time. Mom kept resting her head in her hand. I told her she should lay down. Eileen set up the couch for her with some pillows and I put the pillows under Mom's feet the way she liked them. Eileen looked bewildered and helpless. Mom kept thanking us. When Dad arrived he ran right to Mom. He sat on the couch and bent down to hug her and cried. "How are you doing sweetie?" he said sobbing.

He asked me how she did today. I told him she was fine. I didn't even care that twenty of my guests were in the dining room yacking away without me; the guest of honor sitting at the table with them. I didn't feel rude. I was just worried sick about Mom. She wasn't responding to anything around her. She looked depressed and tired.

When it came time to open up the presents Tamara and Mandy had set up a place for me but I just wanted to open them right next to Mom on the couch. Mom sat up and asked me to put her shoes on.

"What for?" Dad yelled as if she was being silly. "I'm going to be in the pictures," she smiled cheerfully. "I want to look nice for the pictures."

It was amazing how the whole day Mom was exhausted and real quiet and when started opening the presents her face lit up with joy and she commented on every gift. It's like she was alive again. She was laughing and smiling and was so happy for me.

Dad was throwing away the wrapping after each gift. He scolded me for making such a mess. One of the gifts had Bullock's wrapping. When Dad was about to throw it away, Mom said, "No, no, don't throw that away. She can return that."

She was so adorable. She wasn't aware that someone could have heard that. She definitely was not all there.

After I was finished and made my short speech thanking everyone, Mom said "I love you, give me a kiss."

I kissed her lips and hugged her for a long time. I just wanted her to hold me. I cried while I felt Mom's hands gently pat my back. She knew why I was crying. I wanted her to always be there to hold me like that. I was so happy she was able to see all my gifts. Even though she was dying she was so excited for me. It just made me sadder.

She loved me so much that it hurt.

Dad wept as he stared at our embrace. He wasn't just losing his wife, best friend, and the true love of his life; he was also losing the mother of his children. It hurt him to see his children losing their mother. It was all such a mess. Our lives weren't supposed to be this way. We were supposed to be excited to celebrate my wedding. Mom's birthday was coming up. Matt and Tera's one year anniversary was the day after my wedding and Mom and Dad's 30th Anniversary was the day after theirs. We were supposed to be the happiest family with only good things to look forward to and be thankful for. Instead, we were counting the days.

And, Mom was the bravest of all of us.

We sat in the dining room again for the cake. Dad thought he should take Mom home. I ran to the door.

"Bye everybody!" Mom said to all my friends waving and saying with an uncertain tone, "Bye, I'll see you soon!"

As Dad wheeled Mom out, a horrid thought would not leave my mind. I felt that no one in that room would ever see Mom again. I looked at everyone seated at the table and thought of Mom never seeing them again. I thought of her not making it to the wedding. I was getting more and more scared.

Starting tomorrow we were going to have a woman help us with Mom during the day. She wasn't a nurse but she was a homemaker who had a great amount of experience with cancer patients and the terminally ill. She would help Mom with her medication, fix her meals-, etc. Her name was Molly.

I couldn't believe we were actually at the point where we had to resort to outside help from a stranger. It didn't bother Mom one bit. She had such an amazing attitude.

June 4, 1990

I called Dr. Averon from work. I just had to hear for myself what he had to say. I was afraid he wouldn't talk to me, but to my surprise, I was connected to him immediately.

"Hi, Sharon," Dr. Averon said.

I hated his voice as much as I hated his face. I always sensed "bad news" whenever I saw him or heard him. I didn't know what to say. I asked him straight out, "What are my mother's chances of making· it to the wedding?"

Dr. Averon answered in a nonchalant manner, "Well, Sharon, I don't know, it could be three to four weeks. It's touch and go. There's a good chance she will not make it. And even if she is still alive until then there's no telling what condition she'll be in. She's deteriorating rapidly. It's touch and go. That's all I can tell you."

I thanked him for taking the time to talk to me. I felt like it was a lot for him. As soon as I hung up the phone I started crying. I had never cried at work before. I couldn't control my emotions any longer. No matter what, the situation did not look good. Even if Mom did make it to the wedding, it would be a disaster for her. It wouldn't be fair. And to think that my biggest worry a few months ago was that Mom couldn't dance at the wedding. Now, there was a chance she wouldn't even be there!

But the reason I couldn't stop crying was because the bottom line was she was definitely going to die. Wedding or no wedding Mom was dying and there was nothing I could do about it. I wasn't ready to let her go. I just wanted to cling. But like Dad said there is never going to be a time that we are ready to let her go.

Not after the wedding. Not after my first child.

Not after my first house that Mom would help me decorate. I wanted Mom in my life until I could be old with her. After all these years she had finally become my friend, and not just my mother. I needed her so much and I always would.

As soon as I got home from work I ran upstairs. Mom was going to the bathroom and Molly was standing outside the bathroom. I introduced myself to Molly. She seemed to be a very sweet lady. "Who's that?" Mom yelled from the bathroom "Is that Sharon?"

I yelled hello to her and she yelled back, "Hi, sweetie."

Molly left a little later. I laid down next to Mom. Again, she asked me to make sure she was breathing every time she rested her eyes. Matt came over and Mom was so happy to see him but she was so tired. The room was silent. Matt sat there and I was laying next to Mom without saying a word. It was just nice to be together. Anne came over with dinner. She kept asking Mom how their trip was over Memorial weekend. She asked if Mom met any eligible men she could set her up with. Mom said she didn't even notice. Mom didn't even care. I couldn't believe Anne would even think that it was on Mom's mind at the time.

Late that night, Dad walked into the kitchen where I was sitting. Be had just spoken to Carl in New York. Dad looked terrible. He was having such a rough week. I don't think a day went by when he didn't cry his eyes out. He sat at the table with me and let out a big sigh. His face was buried in his hands.

He looked at me and said, "Sharon, I think we are going to have to move-up the wedding. I think we're fooling ourselves."

My heart stopped. "What do you mean?" I asked Dad. "I just spoke to Carl. He thinks I'm fooling myself to think Mom will make it to the wedding. She's getting worse every day."

I tried to remain calm. "So when do you want to move it up?" I heard my voice crack.

Dad said, "As soon as possible, I was thinking next Tuesday, June 12th, that will give us a week to change the arrangements and call all the guests."

I never heard Dad sound so unsure of himself. He always had complete control over any situation and had such confidence. But, I could tell he wasn't sure what he was doing or thinking. I was worried that Mom would lose all her hope if she saw that we were giving up on her. I didn't want to scare her.

Dad felt she wouldn't understand what was going on. She was so out of it that Dad thought she would think it was June 24th anyway. He didn't think she would know the difference.

We talked about our options. I asked if Dad wanted to have it in the backyard. We could cover the pool and put tables over it and there would be enough room for dancing. Dad was set on having it at Sephardic Temple. He would call Jake tomorrow. I would call the rabbi, photographer, the video guy, and all my guests and Tom's.

Dad would call the florist, caterer, band, and all his guests; the New Yorkers first. Dad got up and hugged me real tight. He was sobbing, "I just want so much for you. I love you so much."

I was crying so much I could barely get out the words, "I love you too. He kissed my head and walked away. I could still hear him crying as he walked up the stairs.

I called Tom. I was crying on the phone with him all night. As we talked I stared at the scattered pictures that Sandy took of the shower only two weeks ago. I picked up the close-up of Mom and me. I held it close to my face and started crying hysterically. She looked like she needed me so badly in this picture. Fear was in her eyes. I wanted her to live so badly. I cried and cried.

Tom said firmly, "Honey, I'm coming over!"

I told him he was crazy. It was 2:30 in the morning and he had to be at work in five hours.

"I'm coming over!" he yelled. "You need me right now. I love you. I'll see you in 45 minutes."

Before I could talk him out of it he hung up. Tom was over by 3:30 a.m. I don't think I ever fell asleep. Mom would not leave my mind.

June 5, 1990

I just couldn't sleep. I got up at 6:00 and started making my calls. I called in sick; I felt sick anyway. I didn't get a wink of sleep. I was on the phone all morning with almost all of my friends. They felt awful and were very supportive. All of them offered to help me with the calls, but I wanted to do most of it myself.

When I called the photographer, video guy, etc. they were extremely sympathetic and supportive. Every one of them commented on how special our family was and what a shame it was. They all felt just terrible. It was Mom who found them and hired them. That was the irony of the whole thing. Mom helped plan the entire wedding.

I rescheduled my make-up appointment, hair appointment, manicure. I arranged for Nancy to come to the house so Mom could have her hair and make-up done comfortably. I kept changing the plans from the hotel, to the house, to the temple and back and forth.

I was going out of my mind with these arrangements. I wanted things to be as simple and convenient as possible for Mom. I was afraid she couldn't even handle having her hair and make-up done. I was lost.

I called the bridal shop to tell them I would need my dress ready earlier. They said no problem and were very understanding. I rescheduled my final fitting to today, so the dress would be ready by the end of the week.

Kaye and Tera met me at the bridal shop. They were going to learn how to put up the bustle. When I had the gown on, Kaye and Tera thought it was just beautiful. It just didn't feel right. Mom should have been there putting up the bustle and admiring me in the dress. I was so grateful that I had such a caring family and that Kaye and Tera were there for me.

But I just wanted Mom. It wasn't fair that Mom was missing out on this. It felt so awkward.

Mom was missing· from the picture.

I left the bridal shop feeling very empty. Kaye and Tera went home with me to see Mom. Kaye figured Mom and Dad would be home from the doctor. Mom was laying on the couch with Molly next to her at her feet. Dad looked distressed. We all sat down.

Mom kept saying out of nowhere in a spacy way, "I'm not stupid. I know I'm dying. Why can't I just die?"

"She keeps saying that," Dad told Kaye, as if Mom wasn't there.

"What is wrong with her?" Kaye said in a frustrated tone. "She wasn't this bad two days ago. I just can't believe it." Kaye looked very disturbed by Mom's sudden deterioration.

We all were shocked by it.

Mom went on to say strange things out of context. "Why can't I just cry it out and laugh at all the rest? Everybody dies. Why can't I just die?"

We all sat there stunned murmuring, "Oh, my G-d" to ourselves."

Kaye had to leave to pick up Jennifer. After she left Mom said, "I know why Kaye was here. I'm not stupid."

This was the first time I saw Mom give up. She had accepted her death and was ready to die.

Dad was making his calls to our family and friends regarding the change of the wedding date. He spoke right in front of Mom as if she were incoherent of what was going on.

He would say, "Yeah, it's just not good. We were fooling ourselves thinking she would make it to the wedding. She's deteriorating. It can be any time, we just don't know when…"

Mom sat there giving Dad a funny, strange look as if she thought he was out of his mind. She kept saying, "This is so stupid. Why are you doing this! I'm not going to make it. Just leave it as is. I'm not stupid; I know what's going on. You're so stupid."

But Dad didn't think Mom knew what she was saying. He thought she was oblivious to everything and was just talking nonsense. But, I sincerely thought she was making sense and knew what she was saying. Without a doubt Mom wasn't herself, but I still respected what she had to say whether it made sense or not.

We were all in the kitchen eating a late lunch. I asked Mom if she wanted me to wheel her outside for some fresh hair. She shook her head. "Take me somewhere," she said.

I wheeled her into the den. She said to me, "Are you happy with your decision?"

I said yes.

"It's big," she said.

"What's big?" I asked.

"This decision," she answered.

"Why are you doing this?" she asked me.

I didn't want to say we were doing this because we thought she would die before the 24th. I just said, "Because I want you to walk me down the aisle.

"Now you can name the baby Brittany," Mom said with content.

I burst into tears. She knew she was dying. She was already so sure that she was telling me I could now name my baby after her if it's a girl. Naming my baby after her only meant one thing: that Mom wouldn't be there to see it; her first grandchild from me.

I wheeled Mom back to the kitchen. I was still crying. I said, "She understands. She knows what's going on."

Tera came over to me and hugged me. I told her what Mom had said. I just couldn't stop crying. I was watching Mom die before my eyes. What hurt the most was that she was losing control of her mental state, so I felt as if I had already lost her.

Although she was there physically, the cancer was affecting her brain. I couldn't ask her for advice, I couldn't talk to her about the wedding plans, I couldn't even be sure that she understood me whenever I told her how much I loved her. It hurt so much.

Tom and I spent the rest of the afternoon playing phone tag with our guest list. It was so difficult getting a hold of people and when we did we had to wait for their R.S.V.P. It was so stressful. It was getting out of control.

Thank goodness for the help of our friends. The most frustrating part of it all was all of our New Yorkers. They couldn't let us know if they were coming until they knew they could change their plane reservations. It was making me so anxious. And of course because it was on a Tuesday, it was very difficult for everyone to get away.

To our surprise, everyone was so sympathetic and supportive and all were determined to be at our wedding no matter what it took. We couldn't even begin our table seating arrangements until we had a full R.S.V.P. list.

Tera told me to give Kaye the hotel phone numbers of where Tom and I would be staying in Hawaii. The thought of getting a phone call from Kaye telling us of some horrible news was absolutely frightening. I wanted to right by Mom's side when she died; not catching the first plane home. Sandy suggested we postpone our honeymoon all together since it was so important to me to be home when Mom died. We realized we couldn't enjoy ourselves anyway just dreading that phone call. Most of all, I wanted to spend Mom's last days with her at home, not with me being in Hawaii.

Tera and Matt almost insisted that we go on our honeymoon. Being recent newlyweds themselves, they felt it was very important, especially since we were under such unique circumstances that were very stressful. Tera thought it was important that we spend that time together, alone, and away. Tom probably called our travel agent a dozen times today. We kept changing our minds. Thank goodness he was so understanding. Otherwise he would have thought we were out of our minds.

A lot of wedding gifts were being delivered. Every time I got something, I ran upstairs to tell Mom. I was especially excited that I was receiving so many place settings of our formal china. Mom didn't think we would get all our place settings. I thought she would be pleasantly surprised. But all Mom could say was, "I don't want to hear about it." I knew she didn't mean that. She didn't know what she was saying.

Molly was so great for Mom and Mom really liked her. She would say cute things like, "Molly will take care of that for me, won't you Molly?"

When it was time for Mom's medication Stephen and I ran up to Mom's room at the exact time. But, of course, Molly beat us to it. Molly smiled at us warmly.

Stephen and I had grown so used to giving Mom her medication that it was automatic to go to her room at those particular hours. Mom fiddled around with her pills. It was such an effort for her to take them. It was extremely difficult for her to swallow and six pills was a very big task for her. Molly held them in her hand and Mom touched one and then the other deciding which one to take first. Of course, it didn't make a difference. She just dreaded taking those pills.

It was the Edelstein's turn to come over tonight to bring dinner. Arleen went upstairs to see Mom. She laid down on Mom's bed next to her. "How are you feeling?" Arleen asked Mom.

Mom shrugged her shoulders and made a face. "Stupid question, huh?" Arleen said realizing her foolishness. It was so wonderful that we had so many friends that were like our family that sincerely cared so much. Mom wasn't hungry as usual so Arleen left her alone and went to set up dinner.

Before I was about to leave for the gym, Mom yelled for me. When I got to her room and asked what she needed she just sat there. She didn't say she needed anything. I think she just wanted me. Stephen came up too because our names sound so alike whenever she yelled for us. He thought she was yelling for him.

"Where's Daddy?" Mom asked.

He's at the office we answered.

"Who?" Mom asked with a confused look on her face. "Where's Matt?" Mom asked.

"He's coming over later" we answered.

"Where's Daddy?" Mom asked again.

We said he would be home soon. "Huh?" Mom asked us again with that same confused look.

I think she was just saying words.

"Are you going to the gym?" Mom asked me. I told her I could stay with her.

"You better go to the gym, but visit me before you go, okay, Sharon." She wasn't making sense. I think she just wanted someone nearby.

After dinner I sat with Mom. "It's your birthday next week" I said.

She made a face as if she was saying, "Who cares?" It was as if she wasn't going to live to see her 50th birthday. It was scary. The new wedding date was June 12 and her birthday was June 13. I stood up and just looked at her. She seemed out of it. I started crying very hard. She looked up at me with a confused and sad expression on her face as if she was saying, "Oh, no, don't cry, don't be sad."

I just looked at her and sobbed, "I'm going to be such a good mother because I learned from you. I love you so much."

I bent down to hug her. "We learn from each other." Mom answered.

I cried even more thinking that Mom didn't understand what I told her. Her response was so peculiar. I really felt like I had lost her.

I was crying to Maxine over the phone about Mom. Although Maxine said some very beautiful things in an effort to comfort me, nothing in the world could ease my pain.

I couldn't sleep again. I went into Stephen's room. It was around 1:00 in the morning. Stephen said that in the middle of the night last night Mom got out of bed all by herself, put on her robe, and walked all the way to his room. She turned the light on and woke him up. Then she walked into Dad's office and sat behind his desk saying things that made no sense.

This amazed both of us. For the past week Mom could barely move without our help. Was she sleep walking, we wondered? Tera said it was her brain reacting to habit, not her body. That freaked me out. Dad said that she wasn't sleeping one wink for the past few nights. She was so terrified that if she fell asleep she would never wake up. She was afraid to die. Her eyes would remain wide open all night until the morning. Dad said the other night she got up and put on her clothes and just sat there. When Dad asked what she was doing she said she had somewhere to go.

Well tonight Dad locked their bedroom door from inside so Mom couldn't get out. God forbid, she should fall down the stairs.

That night Stephen and I heard a banging noise. "See, she's doing it again," Stephen said.

We ran to the outside of Mom and Dad's door. Mom was banging on the door screaming, "Joyce! Joyce!"

We heard Dad get a hold of her. He yelled at her like a child, "What are you doing! Get back in bed!"

She yelled, "I have a date with Joyce!" as she continued to play with the door knob.

I asked Stephen who Joyce was and he told me she was Mom's tennis partner from the club. Mom hadn't been able to play tennis since February. I completely forgot about all her tennis friends. It was hard to believe that in the kitchen there was a trophy from a round robin she competed in just in January. And here she was pounding on the door to get out of the house thinking she has a tennis date with Joyce. It was so sad. Dad opened the door and saw us.

He said to us, "Everything is fine. Go to sleep."

This was so strange. Where did Mom get all this energy to get up, get dressed and walk to the door all by herself? Where did she think she was going? If the door wasn't locked and we let her out, what would have happened? Where would she have gone? I was sure her brain was swelling from all the dirty blood in her body since her liver wasn't functioning. I was so scared for her.

June 6, 1990

I called the office and told Susan what was going on. She was very understanding. She even said she would tell Dan what was happening. I couldn't keep calling in sick. I told Susan I would definitely be back tomorrow.

Tom and I went downtown today to get our marriage license and wedding rings. We mounted my engagement stone into the wedding ring setting. It was just exquisite. I was so excited for Mom to see it. She was the one who found this setting and was so enthused about it. To see it done was so exciting.

We went next door to buy Tom a ring. This wasn't what we had planned. Tom had planned to spend the next couple of weeks looking carefully for a ring but we had no choice. We had to buy one today. I took him to the jeweler where Mom and I had seen that ring for Tom. To my amazement, out of all the hundreds of rings on display, Tom picked out the one Mom had seen last April. I looked through my purse to see if I still had that business card with the style number on it. Sure enough, it was the exact ring that Mom had picked out. Tom and I were so surprised and excited over this amazing coincidence. I just couldn't wait to show Mom our rings. She was going to be so happy and shocked that Tom picked out that same ring.

When Tom and I got our marriage license, it really hit me that we were getting married in six days and Mom was going to see it! She would be at our wedding and it was going to be just wonderful!

When we got home, I ran up the stairs to see Mom. After thinking a lot about it, I decided that it would be best to not show Mom the rings yet. This was because I thought she would get suspicious over why we got them so early when, in her mind, the wedding was June 24. I wasn't sure if she had lost her perception of time, but my primary concern was to not frighten her. I didn't want Mom to know the wedding was moved up to June 12. I wanted her to think it was "June 24th" the day of our wedding. I didn't want Mom to think that we thought she wouldn't live to see June 24th. I felt that if she saw us giving up then she would give up.

Tom and I sat with Mom. "It's going to be so beautiful" Tom said of the wedding.

"I don't want to hear about it Tom" Mom answered. That wasn't like her. She was really losing her mind. She would never talk to Tom that way. She was always nicer to him than she even was to me.

It was Cheryl and Hal Gold's turn to come over with dinner. During dinner, Mom was eating very little. I noticed that as she ate she had a grin on her face and was staring at something.

I don't know if she was looking out the window or just staring into space. But that grin would not leave her face. I wondered if she was ready to go. I was so curious.

After dinner Dad asked Mom, "What do you want to do now, dear?"

"Dance." She said.

We all laughed at her sarcastic answer to Dad's silly question. Even while she knew she was dying she made us laugh. She had the best sense of humor of anyone I had ever known.

Hal sat with Dad while Cheryl and I sat upstairs with Mom. Cheryl had such a gentle way with Mom. Mom had to go the bathroom so we both helped her. Mom sat there and kept saying, "Wait a minute."

Cheryl stroked her back and said, "Take your time, honey. We're not going anywhere."

Mom looked so helpless. Cheryl looked at me and said sweetly, "She was such a beautiful Mommy. It's such a shame. It's not fair."

I wanted to cry. "I know," I said softly."

We were in the bathroom with Mom for a while. I was in my gym clothes because I was planning on going to a 7:30 class. I decided to forget about it. Mom needed me. Cheryl said, "Why don't you go. You've been with her all day. I'll take care of her. Go ahead."

I felt so disloyal leaving. Before I left, I went back to Mom's room. Cheryl had gone downstairs. I stood at the doorway in shock over what I saw. Dad was sitting at the edge of the bed and Mom was sitting in the chair across from him, getting up and sitting down several times walking in circles, completely fidgety. She was making moaning and groaning sounds. She kept pulling huge patches out of her hair as she walked in circled.

Dad said lovingly, "Leave your hair alone dear."

She sat on Dad's lap and gave him a big hug. She held his head against her chest and squeezed him as she gently rocked him like a little baby. Dad started weeping.

"You want to sit on me, sweetie? Alright darling you can sit on me" he said to her as if she was a little girl.

They held each other tight as Mom couldn't keep still and continued to make funny sounds. Dad kept crying as he she hugged him. It was the most loving, yet most devastating sight I had ever seen. It was as if Mom was saying good-bye to Dad. She just knew she was dying. She hadn't hugged him like that in so long.

I couldn't bare to look anymore. Dad didn't see me in the doorway and I didn't know what to do, so I left. During the drive to the gym, I started to feel real sick. I had a pounding headache and my stomach was upset. During the class, I felt light headed. Something just wasn't right. I felt faint.   ,

On the drive home Barbra Streisand sang, "The Way We Were" on the radio. This was the opening theme song on Mom and Dad's 25th anniversary video. I started crying thinking about their storybook romance. The words were so beautiful, yet heart breaking.

The one part of the song that always got to me was, "Smiles we gave to one another, for the way we were." Those words seemed to be the story of my childhood. Mom's warm smile loving me for who I was.

I had to get out of this depression. I felt good about going back to work tomorrow. Everything was pretty under control and most of the plans were reorganized. I was still a major stress case, but I just had to go back to work.

When I got home, I noticed Matt and Tera's car was in the driveway. I opened the front door to see Dad at the top of the stairs as if he was waiting for me. I could hear Mom groaning upstairs. Before I was half way up the stairs Dad said looking at me with tears in his eyes, "We have to take Mom to the hospital. I'm sorry dear."

He wept as he hugged me in the middle of the stair case. "I'm so sorry," he sobbed. "We tried."

I felt my body sweat. I didn't know if it was from the gym, from Dad, or just this horrible tragedy. My nightmare had come true. My hopes, prayers and dreams were shattered. The last thing we wanted to do was take Mom to the hospital. How could Dr. Averon do this to us? We had asked if we should have a nurse be with Mom so she could die at home. But he said it wasn't necessary. And here we were taking Mom to the hospital.

When I got to the top of the stairs I hugged Matt as we both cried. I asked what had happened. Tera said Mom was very agitated and kept screaming that she was dying. When Dad called Dr. Averon and he heard Mom in the background screaming that she was dying, he said to Dad, "She's right; she's dying. Take her to the hospital."

Tera was furious with Dr. Averon. Mom and Dad were just at his office this morning. He had Dad refill all of Mom's prescriptions today. Dad said the strangest thing of all was that Dr. Averon did not schedule Mom for another appointment. The first time in six years he just simply didn't schedule her to come back next week. He must have known she was dying. Mom certainly knew it but she had me fooled.

I fooled myself.

We paced around Mom and Dad's room as we waited for the ambulance. Mom was so restless. "When are they getting here!?" Mom yelled.

Mom had to go the bathroom. Matt was going to take her. I took Mom's hands out of Matt's so I could take her. Tera came with me. Mom was shaking and sweating and breathing heavy.

"Oh, my G-d!!!" she kept yelling.

I kept saying, "Okay Mommy, let's go Mommy." I hadn't called her Mommy since I was little.

When we got her to the toilet, I stroked her back. She was groaning and kept saying, "Oh, G-d." She was literally dying before our eyes. I couldn't believe it was happening. She looked like she was in excruciating pain. I had no idea how she physically felt when she screamed that she was dying. It frightened me.

I followed Tera into my room. She called Rabbi Shuman but he wasn't home so she spoke to his wife. Tera said, "It's almost time, we would like Rabbi Shuman to do the funeral. Will he be available tomorrow or the next day?"

I couldn't believe I was hearing this. I couldn't believe the end was so near.

When the ambulance got to our house, Mom sat in the chair across from her bed. She flopped up her arms as if the gesture meant, "Sorry guys, I tried."

It felt odd to have two paramedics in our house. They put Mom in a stretcher took her down the stairs and out of our lives.

As they were setting up the ambulance to get her in, she kept saying impatiently, "Let's go already." She was so calm. She just wanted to go.

The paramedics asked if she needed anything before they left for the hospital. "Water," she said.

I ran into the house to get a small bottle of Evian. As I ran down the driveway to give it to her, my heart sank. She looked so helpless waiting for these paramedics to take her away.

Before they got her in the back, Stephen gave her a kiss and said, "Good-bye Mommy," as if this was final.

Dad got in the back of the ambulance with Mom.

We all went back into the house. As we were about to leave Matt said someone should go upstairs to turn out the lights in Mom and Dad's bedroom. I said I would do it. It was more difficult than I imagined.

I cried intensely as I turned off the lamp on Mom's nightstand. Her slippers were on the floor beside her bed as if she had just stepped out of them. Her cane was leaning against the nightstand. I stared at her side of the bed and sobbed. Then I stared at Dad's side of the bed. How was he going to sleep in this bed ever again without Mom? She would not only never wear those slippers again, never use that cane again and never sleep in that bed again. She would never step foot in this house again; never be in my life again.

I cried and cried at this tragic reality. I wept more when I went into the bathroom to turn those lights off. I looked at the toilet, the shower, the tub, her make-up, her things. I just could not believe she wasn't coming back. I knew everybody could hear me crying. Stephen met me at the top of the stairs and hugged me as we both cried in each other's arms. Tera and Matt looked up at us from downstairs. My body was shaking.

Matt, Tera, Stephen and I drove to the hospital together. Tom and Julia were probably already at the hospital. While I was at the gym, Stephen had called Tom to ask where I was. Tom paged me at the gym and Julia happened to be at the gym so she answered the page. Tom told Julia they would drive to the hospital together. I must have been driving home when Tom tried to page me. Tom had known about Mom before I did.

When we got the hospital Mom was in her room groaning agonizing sounds from the pain. It hurt so much to see her like this. Mom could not keep still in her bed. She kept throwing the blankets off of her and kept trying to sit up. She kept screaming, "Give me a shot! Where's Dr. Averon?" Her voice did not even sound like her own anymore. It was real deep and hoarse.

"I need a shot!!" Mom kept hollering. She was in excruciating pain. I kept trying to calm her down. I stroked her hair and tried to get her to lay down but she was so restless. She was raving. I didn't even recognize her.

"Where's Dr. Averon?" Mom yelled again.

We were all trying to comfort her but nothing could help her. She was out of control. "I'm peeing!" she screamed.

Tera helped wipe her off. Just as Tera was wiping her leg Tom was at the doorway.

"Get out of here Tom!" Mom screamed. We were so surprised that Mom had the energy to scream that loud. I ran out to talk to Tom. He was huddled against the wall crying hysterically. He knew Mom didn't mean anything. She loved him so much. Tom knew it was the awkward timing. She was in such an embarrassing position when Tom walked in. We all knew it but it still hurt a lot.

Matt came out to tell Tom that he should actually be flattered that Mom recognized him and screamed his name out considering the state she was in. I didn't want "Get out of here Tom!" to be the last words Mom said to Tom. I kept trying to get Tom to back in the room but there didn't seem to be an appropriate time.

After we were there for about twenty minutes Dr. Averon finally showed up. I saw him walking down the hall. All I could think was that I never wanted to see his face again. He went in to see Mom.

Later, he gathered all of us. He said, "She's very agitated and in a lot of pain. Her liver isn't functioning. The medication I can give her to make her less agitated needs to be taken by someone with a healthy liver. Now, since her liver is failing this medication can kill her."

He looked at Dad and said, "If you do not want us to revive her I need you to sign some papers tonight." We all agreed.

Then to my surprise he said they would try and pull her through Tuesday for the wedding. He was going to have a liver specialist come in the morning. What the hell was he doing now? Giving us another false sense of hope? What could a liver specialist do at this point, besides add another hunk to the bill? I was even more upset when Tom told me he had heard a conversation between Dr. Averon and the nurse.

The nurse said, "Liver failure, huh?" and Dr. Averon said "She has about 24 hours."

We all sat in the visitor's lounge down the hall. We felt so helpless. I wanted to be with Mom anyway so I went in there alone. Dr. Averon left.

Mom was screaming for him again. "Where did he go?" she yelled. She knew he wasn't coming back. She was still screaming for the shot. They were going to give it to her later. I was surprised how brave she was. She knew that if they gave her something she would probably never regain consciousness. But, she was in so much pain.

The nurse came in to put a catheter in so mom could go to the bathroom. As I was about to leave the room, Mom said something I couldn't really hear.

The nurse said, "She said 'stay.' She wants you to stay.

I was so happy she wanted me with her.

The nurse asked, "Is this your Mom?" I sadly said, "Yes." The nurse nodded.

Mom was like a little kitten when the nurse inserted the device in her. I told Mom she was so brave. She didn't seem to care. I went back into the lounge.

It was already 10:30 p.m. and we were starving. Well, I was definitely not going back to work tomorrow. I had really planned on in too. While Dad went to sign the papers, the rest of us went to the disgusting cafeteria to eat. It was the six of us; Tom, me, Matt, Tera, Stephen and Julia. I thought of how Mom and Dad's three children multiplied into six children and Mom wasn't going to enjoy her six children and grandchildren. I was so sad.

I had no appetite. Of course the food was probably what got a lot of the patients in the hospital to begin with. It felt nice to be with each other. I thought of how Mom told us she wanted us to stick together and be there for each other, especially for Dad. He was going to need our support. But, nothing in the world was going to heal our grief. I couldn't eat a thing without feeling sick.

When we went back to Mom's room she was breathing heavy, groaning sighs. She was asleep and they gave her the shot. The nurse said that even though her breaths were moans she was not in any pain. She was sleeping. She looked so helpless and not at peace. I watched her body move with each struggling breath she took and all I could think of was that I never said good-bye.

I had told her that I loved her and how much she meant to me. But, I never told her how much I would miss her. I guess it was my way of not letting her think that I was giving up on her. I was so naive. I should have known that she knew she was dying. I was always trying to protect her by letting her think that I didn't know how sick she was. I figured she would keep fighting. But of course she knew I had an idea. I just never admitted to myself that she would die. I never believed it until now.

Dad looked at us and said, "Well there's nothing we can do now, we might as well go home." It was already 11:30 p.m. but I didn't want to leave her. There was really nothing for us to do. Dad drove home with us. I had forgotten he didn't have his car because he drove with Mom in the ambulance.

Dad told us, "She hugged me today." He started crying. "She hadn't hugged me in such a longtime. It was beautiful." I knew that that hug was Mom's farewell hug to Dad. I just knew it.

Matt and Tera said goodbye to Dad in the driveway. They asked if he would be okay and offered to sleep over. We were worried about him sleeping alone. Dad said Stephen was going to sleep with him tonight and that made us feel better.

Dad cried, "I feel so guilty leaving her there all alone, I never wanted her in the hospital." None of us did. Dad and I closed the front door and held each other and cried. "I'm so sorry, dear," Dad said. "I love you so much."

I sat with Dad at the kitchen table while he ate a snack. I didn't know how he could eat. I had completely lost my appetite. I asked him what we were going to do if Mom was to live until Tuesday and what would we do if she died tonight? I was filled with guilt for thinking of myself at a time like this but the wedding would not leave my mind just as much as Mom would not leave my mind. I just had to know.

Dad looked sad and said, "I'm sorry dear. I can't have anything." I asked if we could have a small ceremony in the backyard. Dad said, "I'm so sorry-darling. You and Tom will have to elope. I just can't do anything. I wanted this for you so much. We tried. I want everything for you." He stroked my hair and cried. "I'm so sorry dear."

He went upstairs. My stomach was turning and my heart felt like it stopped. I had a huge lump in my throat. Then I burst into hysterical tears. I just could not believe this tragedy was happening. I went to my room and cried and cried and cried. I heard a knock at my door. It was Dad standing there crying. I didn't know he could hear me crying like that. I didn't want him to hear me so hysterical. I hugged him and told him I was sorry. He said, "I wish I could have something for you but I just can't." I told him I understood but I couldn't stop crying. I felt ashamed of myself for the way I was acting. Here was Dad standing at my door, concerned about me because I was crying, while poor Mom was dying in the hospital.

Dad had so much love in him that he could worry about hurting me even while he was losing the other half of his life. He was just as devoted of a father as he was a husband. It tore me up inside to see Dad in such pain. He was the most beautiful person and this had to be happening to him. I didn't want to make things worse for him. What was I doing to him? I cried into my pillow the rest of the night so he couldn't hear me. Tom and I were on the phone all night again. We decided we would call Rabbi Shuman first thing in the morning. It was 3:00 in the morning so that was really in a few hours. I never fell asleep.

June 7, 1990

I called Tera at 7:00 in the morning. I knew she would be up. I told her how confused I was. I just didn't know what I should do. If Mom lived until Tuesday, June 12, I didn't know if we should go on with the wedding as planned. Tera said, "Sharon, Mom is going to die any minute." She was right. What was I thinking? There was no way she would live until Tuesday.

Tera felt that Tom and I should get married in the rabbi's study. I just cried and cried over that idea.

Tera said, "Sharon, every girl has a dream of being a bride, wearing a beautiful gown and walking down the aisle. But your dreams were shattered. You were cheated. The time in your life that should have been so special for you turned out to be a tragedy and you just have to deal with that." I felt like I just couldn't.

Tom and I called Tera's father who was also our Cantor. I told him everything Dad had said; that we should just elope. He just couldn't handle any kind of wedding. Our Cantor said that the time I spoke to was the worst time for all of us. Dad was in such a painful state that he probably couldn't think straight. All he was thinking of was that his wife was dying. Our Cantor said, maybe later, his head would be clearer. He said we should get married in the rabbi's study on Tuesday and that I shouldn't wear my gown.

I asked why not and he said, "Sharon, how could you wear a white gown while your mother lays in her grave?" All I could do was cry. He said that one of the Ten Commandments is to "honor thy father," and that was what we had to do. We knew how much pain Dad was in and the last thing in the world I wanted to do was hurt him or make the pain worse.

We were all hurting. I was willing to do whatever Dad felt most comfortable with but I just couldn't elope like he said. We then called Rabbi Shuman three-way. He said the situation was very unfortunate, but there was nothing we could do.

I asked if it would be proper to have a quiet small ceremony in our backyard without music. He said as long as what we did didn't offend or hurt other people it was okay. But, he also felt I couldn't wear my gown.

Nobody seemed to understand what I was feeling. I called Kaye. She felt terrible. "This is such a tragedy," she said, "Everything is ruined for you. I feel so awful."

I told her what the Cantor and the Rabbi had said. Kaye couldn't believe it. She said, "But, Bernice wouldn't have wanted that! Your mother said she wanted you to go on with the wedding as planned. She wouldn't want it any other way. Of course, you should wear your gown. Mom picked it out. This is what she wanted. These were her wishes. Your mother told me."

That was just the kind of mother Mom was. She knew she was dying yet still had the same genuine concern for me and the never ending care. Even though she wouldn't be alive to see it, she still wanted my happiness. It hurt even more to let her go.

She was the most beautiful person.

I cried to Kaye and said I just didn't know what to do and what hurt the most was that I needed to ask Mom what I should do and for the first time in my life she wasn't there.

"Oh, I'm so sorry," Kaye said. "I just know she would want you to have this wedding, she told me."

I just kept thinking of what I had just told Kaye. I needed Mom's advice and she wasn't there to guide me. I needed to hear her wishes from her own voice. I needed to see her reassurance in her eyes. I couldn't face the reality that I never would again. It hurt so much. She was always there to help me with all my petty problems.

And now this tragedy.

All my life she guided me through those tragedies too. At the time when I needed her most she wasn't there. I felt so lost. I felt guilty, sad, confused, and devastated. I just wanted Mom.

And she was on the brink of death.

Dad told me Molly came over for Mom this morning. When Dad told her she was in the hospital and to not come back tomorrow she started crying. It was so touching that this sweet lady who only cared for Mom for three days was heartbroken that she would never see her again. It was just a reflection of how much Mom touched people's hearts. Even a person who only knew her for three days was crying for her. Dad paid Molly for the rest of the week anyway. She took such good care of her.

I called everyone I felt I could talk to. I called Sara at work. She asked how Mom knew she was dying yesterday. We imagined how frightening it must feel.

Sara said when she talked to her boss about all this and Sara said, "I guess things happen for a reason." Her boss told her, "No, it's not for a reason. My brother was brutally murdered when his home was robbed. There is no reason for that. There is no reason why your friend's mother should suffer and die this way. There isn't a reason for everything."

There were just no easy answers.

It was still very early in the morning. Around 9:00 I called work to let them know what was happening. I was fortunate that they were so understanding and supportive. Tom was going to come over around 10:00 so we could go to the hospital together. It was already 10:30 and he still wasn't over. Feeling so vulnerable, I had horrible thoughts. If this could be happening to Mom then anything was bound to happen to Tom. I mean why not? I felt so gullible to think that nothing tragic could ever happen to me or my family. How could it? We were good people. This was such a lesson for me. Anything can happen to anybody no matter how special someone is. I just always thought G-d was magical and nothing terrible could ever happen to us. I always felt protected and safe. But, I was wrong.

I guess I was going out of my mind because Tom was taking so long to get there. I wandered and paced around the house. Mom was everywhere. It was funny how I never realized how much everything in the house was her until that moment. Her beauty, elegance, taste, style, class, cheerfulness, and perfection was all over the house. Every corner, every wall, every room, there she was.

I found it hard to accept that she would never walk through the door again and go up to her room, or go into her kitchen, or just be in this dream house that she and Dad finally bought convinced that Mom would live. I reflected back on how every time they were close to buying a new house Mom would think it wasn't the right thing to do since wasn't going to live. But, when they bought this house it reassured all of us that she would live. This was the house that Mom and Dad were supposed to retire in together with their children coming over for Sunday brunches, grandchildren celebrating birthday parties and friends coming over for summer barbeques.

I simply could not accept it.

Mom's wheelchair was still at the bottom of the staircase. Just as if she had just gotten out of it. It was hard to believe that Matt and Stephen brought that wheelchair through the door only four days ago. And we thought we'd be wheeling around Mom for a couple more months.

At least I fooled myself into thinking that.

Tom finally got there. By the time I called the hospital it was already 11:30. Matt answered the phone. I asked how Mom was and Matt said with his voice cracking, "You better get here quick."

My body began to shake. My biggest fear at that moment was that Mom would die without me there. I would never forgive myself. I had to be there. Tom and I ran down the stairs. Since I hadn't eaten a thing, Tom forced me to bring something to eat in the car. I had absolutely no appetite whatsoever. I grabbed an apple and filled an empty Evian bottle with apple juice too oblivious to realize how stupid it was to have an apple with apple juice.

Tom drove faster than I had ever seen before. My hands were shaking so much I couldn't even hold the apple and the bottle so I put them down. Tom was trying to get me to take a bite of the apple. I took one little bite and felt ill. All I could think of was Mom not being alive. She just had to hold on for me at least until we got there.

I prayed that she was still alive. By the time we parked at the hospital I was shaking so much that Tom carried me in. He was running carrying me in his arms all the way to the elevator. It was as if he was rushing me to the hospital.

My heart was racing while the elevator stopped at Mom's floor. I ran down the hall and could see Matt from far away. His arms were folded and he looked sullen. I gave him a hug and asked what was happening. "Her blood pressure's dropping," he cried.

I went in to Mom's room to see her hooked up to a respirator. She was on her own with no machines, struggling to take every next breath of life. Her head nodded with every breath she took. She was hanging on for her life. The saddest part about the whole thing was that she was in a coma. Dad, Grandma, and Leo were in the little visitor's room across the hall.

I hugged Dad and cried. He was crying too. "I'm so sorry for the way I was carrying on last night," I sobbed.

"It's alright dear, I love you, I'll do anything you want" Dad said, crying.

I hugged Grandma. She was sobbing. "I know, I know," I whispered in her ear.

I knew what she was feeling. Mom was her little girl that she never had. Grandma had known Mom since she was only sixteen. I kept hearing Grandma's voice in my head. Those words of, "I don't want to see Mommy until she is better. It breaks my heart to see her so sick, I'll see her when she is better."

No wonder Mom was so persistent in getting Grandma to go to my shower on Sunday. She wanted to say goodbye.

I asked Dad how long Mom had been in a coma. Dad said since last night, right after they gave her that medication. "We've lost her. She's gone," Dad said crying.

I finally accepted that there wasn't going to be any miracle and Mom really was gone. It just wasn't "official." I noticed that Stephen wasn't there, he was actually at work. Matt was angry and called him to tell him to get to the hospital. Stephen felt that Mom was gone, and he said good-bye to her last night. Matt sternly said he should be there with his family. Stephen was there a few hours later.

I went in and out of Mom's room feeling helpless. I put my face over hers and said, "Mom, I love you, I love you Mom." She moaned a little and I prayed I wasn't just hearing things. Tom said he saw her respond too.

Lee arrived with Aunt Barb and Uncle Nolan. They came directly from the airport. Nolan stroked Mom's forehead, and said, "Bern, it's me, Nolan."

I could have sworn I saw Mom's left eyebrow raise. But, that could have just been from Nolan stroking her forehead. I wondered if she could hear us, or sense us in her room. Roz said the nurse said she was aware of her surroundings.

I wanted to believe it. I thought it was so cute how Nolan called his little sister, "Bern." They had a very special bond. I reflected back on how when Nolan was in California in February and Mom screamed before he left our house for the airport. She had a premonition that she would never see him again. And here we were less than four months later, and Mom proved that she knew her fate.

It was frightening to think of how scared Mom must have been. She always seemed so strong to me that I never saw her fear. She must have been terrified all those months but she never let me know it. I just saw her strong will to live and to me she was a fighter. She was still fighting.

I was wandering the hall going from Mom's room to the little visitor's room to the visitor's lounge just going in circles like a zombie. I felt so helpless, devastated and lost with confusion. I didn't want to let go of Mom but I knew I had no choice.

As I moped down the hall I barely noticed Sandy walking towards me. As soon as I saw her I started crying. She held me and I sobbed in her arms. Just having her there brought out my emotions. Here I was losing my mother in the room right next to us and there was my future mother in-law comforting me as I cried on her shoulder. It was so overwhelming for me. Dad cried when Sandy went to hug him. We all ended up in the bigger visitor's lounge.

Uncle Nolan said to Sandy, "That's my baby sister in there."

"I know," Sandy said softly.

Dad looked at me and stroked my hair. He was crying and said to me, "You're so pale."

I know, I looked sick myself. I hadn't slept in days, hadn't eaten much, my eyes were puffy and red from crying, and my hair was stringy. Of course I looked pale. I felt pale.

Sandy talked about losing her twelve year-old brother when she was nine years old. She talked about letting go. Sandy never said goodbye to her brother. She and Dad talked about the wedding. Dad looked at me with tears in his eyes and said, "We'll do something dear. I don't know what, but we'll do a little something."

I was so exhausted and depressed. Tom drove me to his house so I could take a shower and change my clothes. Tom called Paul to tell him to cancel all the Vegas plans for his bachelor party that was supposed to be that weekend. They had already put down money on the rooms and people had bought tickets and everything. But, they would just have to understand. Tom didn't care at all. This was nothing.

I felt fresher after my shower but I still felt awful. When we got back to the hospital Selma was there and so were Roz and Sherri.

Selma said to me, "Your Dad tells me that you and Mom spent some precious time together over the weekend and I can see a special bond between you and your Dad that I never saw before."

Selma would know. She and Mom had been friends since birth. Selma watched me grow up. She and Mom experienced everything together. They had the funniest stories from their childhood. They were always laughing hysterically whenever they got together.

I was standing with Aunt Barb at the foot of Mom's bed. She looked so vulnerable. I felt so helpless. Aunt Barb said, "Bernice's hands are so beautifully manicured. Just beautiful."

I stared at Mom's bands. They were always beautiful. Her manicure was so fresh. Her nails were so long and the nail polish was still perfect. She had just gotten a manicure five days ago. It was bizarre to look at how healthy and strong her nails were while the rest of her body was wasting away. How could that be possible?

I looked at my hands.

We had the same shaped hands and the exact fingers and nails. I held her hand in mine. I expected her hand to be ice cold but it wasn't. I knew she couldn't feel me or hear me. I felt like I had lost her.

We all wanted to go to dinner but we were afraid to leave Mom. We all just had to be by her side when she died. We dreaded the thought of coming back from dinner and being told that she was gone. We went anyway but we were real nervous. We walked across the street to Hamburger Hamlet. There were about twenty of us.

I had the strangest feeling. For the first time ever in my life we were going out to dinner without Mom. The feeling was so empty. It felt so wrong, so out of place. I felt like we were abandoning Mom. I looked across the street at the hospital tower and thought of her in her room fighting for her life while we were going out to dinner. I knew I would have to get used to it. This was only going to be the first of many dinners without her.

The first of many moments without her.

On the walk over, Uncle Lonny asked me what we were going to do about the wedding. He thought we should go on and have it on June 24th. "Forget this June 12 business. Forget you ever changed the date," he said.

I didn't know what was going to happen. I just wished I could have asked Mom what to do. But, that was impossible. I was so miserable I didn't even have an appetite. Aunt Barb kept telling me to eat. It reminded me of when I was little.

She probably thought I never changed. On the walk back Uncle Lonny said to Tom, "So how long do you plan on using this as an excuse to not go to work?"

Tom was so shocked he didn't even know how to respond. He said something to the effect that he wouldn't go back until Mom died, that he had a wedding to plan and I needed him. This wasn't an excuse. I couldn't believe Uncle Lonny would say something like that.

As we approached the ugly Cedar Sinai building my stomach was turning. I was afraid of what I would find up there. We weren't gone for long. It was about 7:45 p.m. Thank goodness Mom was still alive. I stood right beside her with Aunt Barb. Dad, Uncle Nolan, Lee and Roz were on the other side.

I watched helplessly as Mom struggled to breath every breath. She opened her eyes just a little bit and I think she saw me. I noticed the intervals in between her breaths were becoming longer. She was breathing slower.

I thought of last weekend when Mom kept asking me to make sure she was breathing each time she laid her head on her pillow. Mom's voice was ringing in my head; "Make sure I'm breathing, okay Sharon? You'll make sure I'm breathing, right?"

I wasn't going to stop caring for her now. Her breathing became irregular and there were long gasps and little gasps. I then noticed that she didn't take another breath after the last one from before.

She wasn't breathing at all.

Aunt Barb turned to me and exclaimed, "She stopped breathing! Did you see that?"

She called over the nurse and told her she was not breathing. As the nurse checked Mom, Aunt Barb held on to me. Dad approached Mom as the nurse checked her. The nurse had to let us know it was official. But, I knew she was gone. It was over.

Dad cried to the nurse, "Take this off," as he gently took Mom's respirator off her face. Dad was treating Mom as if she could still feel the discomfort of the respirator even though he knew she was no longer living.

Uncle Nolan left the room to gather everyone up. Tom, Stephen and Matt motioned me to stand with them. There were probably twelve of us surrounding Mom. We all held hands at the foot of the bed.

The nurse looked at all of us and nodded her head. It was true. Mom was dead. With everybody crying and carrying on we sounded like suffering, howling animals.

The cries and sobs seemed to echo throughout the whole room. Even the nurse shed a tear and she saw this a few times a day.

Dad went over to Mom and was crying uncontrollably. He kneeled down beside her bed and laid his body across Mom's chest.

He cried, "Sleep peacefully, darling, I'll see you soon."

Matt cried out, "Dad!"

I knew Dad didn't mean that as a death wish. He meant, "Someday." It was beautiful, yet heartbreaking.

Stephen and I stood beside Mom's bed. I brushed a stray hair off her yellow-gray face and kissed her cheek. Her mouth was still wide open from that last breath of life.

She didn't look at peace. She looked sad. The way I read her face, I sensed that she had more to say, things to do, grandchildren to see, days to live.

It felt so wrong, beyond comprehension. It made no sense. It was strange to stare at someone's face for that long and not see life and to only hear silence. It was even stranger that this first dead person I had ever seen was my own mother. It felt like it just couldn't be happening. It was a true nightmare that I was praying to wake up from. But, it wasn't a dream and I was definitely awake. This was my life.

It didn't even look like her. She looked like a corpse not Mom. I just kept staring at her face in disbelief and shock. "She was so beautiful," I said. "She doesn't even look like her."

Dad said, "She was always beautiful and we will remember her the way she was. She never stopped being beautiful." Dad was right.

Stephen kissed her forehead and was stroking the side of her face. He started crying and hysterically sobbing, "This can't be my mommy! This can't be my mommy!"

I was in so much pain that I was numb. I couldn't even cry anymore. Matt and Tera were in the small visitor's room on their knees holding each other and unable to stop crying. Stephen and I were such zombies that Tom and Julia ended up holding each other and crying.

We were waiting for Dr. Averon to confirm Mom's death. He had to make it official. I sat in the chairs against the wall beside Mom's bed with Dad, Selma and Lee.

Dad cradled me with his arm. His tired body was soaked with sweat. Dr. Averon checked Mom. He then looked at Dad and said, "She's no longer suffering."

I knew I would be hearing that uncomforting, good for nothing line many times to come. Dad stood up and gave Dr. Averon a big hug. "Thank you for taking care of her," Dad cried.

I had to admit, the man did keep Mom alive for six beautiful, unforgettable years that we would treasure. Dr. Averon confirmed Mom's time of death as 8:10 p.m. although I saw her die at 7:55.

Dad said that she could have kept us there until midnight but she died as soon as we came back. She didn't want to keep us waiting. Dad said, "She cared about us so much. Even in dying she cared about us." It was so true. Mom waited for all of us to be there when she died.

She was as unselfish in death as she was in life.

She could have died while we were at dinner but she didn't want to die alone.

I thought of how she opened her eyes a little and saw Barb and me and maybe everyone else who was surrounding her. Maybe that made her decide she was ready to die; we were all there with her. She couldn't have drifted out of our lives more beautifully.

It still hurt so much.

We just sat there staring at Mom's body. I couldn't believe she was gone. Lee and Anthony went over and covered her with the blanket over her head.

"Just leave her!" Dad shouted. "They'll take care of everything."

Tom and I thought that was so silly. You always see that in movies. We knew she was dead. There was no need to cover her face. The morticians were on their way to pick her up.

There was nothing left for us to do but it was too hard to just leave. Since Tom drove me to the hospital I went with Matt and Tera. As we pulled out of the parking lot I looked up at the tower. I couldn't believe Mom was actually gone forever. I told Matt and Tera I could still hear her voice.

How was Dad going to sleep alone tonight? He wasn't going to have Stephen sleep with him again because he said he had to get used to it.

We all were going to have to get used to this void. I was at the point where I couldn't even cry anymore. I cried all the tears I had for that day. My eyes were so red and dry and I was so emotionally drained. I still felt like this couldn't be happening.

The person that gave me life was gone, just like that.

I would never see her again.

I would never laugh with her again.

I would never hear her soothing voice.

I could still smell her sweet breath of her kisses.

I wouldn't let myself let go of her.

I went to sleep that night hoping I would see her in my dreams.

* * * * * *

Epilogue

What you just read was exactly as it was written when I was twenty-four years old. Nearly twenty-eight years ago when I recorded my feelings and memories about my mother's passing it was never my intention to make a book or to share these words with an audience. These thoughts and memories were for myself; for my own personal journey and my healing. In fact, I considered my thoughts very private and out of respect for my grieving father, wanted to protect our family's privacy.

So why share it now?

As I began to approach the age of my mother's death and my children became the same ages as my brothers and me when we lost her, it dawned on me how very young my mother was when she died. I thought, "If I'm lucky enough to live past her age, I promise I will make every day count and truly celebrate life."

When I actually did reach the age of fifty, the feeling for me was bitter-sweet. I had survived past my mother's forty-nine year lifespan, six days shy of her fiftieth birthday. This milestone brought me to the realization that life is precious, just as my father once said to my mother, "We are only here for a visit."

Walking the footsteps that my mother never had a chance to take has instilled in me the purpose to live a life of meaning. I wanted to share my story with others so that they too would treasure loved ones and cherish the memories of those who have passed. This was among my mother's wishes: to speak of her, to share stories of her, to remember her.

It is my hope that after reading this book, you will live life fully and with meaning as well, and always honor the memory of those you have lost.

I love you Mom.

I miss you every day.

You're forever in my heart.

The author was born Sharon Lisa Elbaum in 1966, Brooklyn, New York. She graduated from U.C.L.A. in 1988 with a Bachelor's degree in Sociology with an emphasis in Business Administration.
Sharon is the proud mother of three adult children including two sons and one daughter.
She resides in Southern California where she is currently working on her next book.

Acknowledgement

Thank you Mike for your editing and forward statement assistance. The publishing of this book would not have come to fruition without your support, belief in me, your encouragement, and the guiding light you are in my life.

Made in the USA
Middletown, DE
06 May 2018